EXTRO•

INTROSPECTION   NEUTRASPECTION

EXTROSPECTION   ACTION ™

DYNAMICS

2nd Edition (Revised)

The power of *Practical Compassion in ACTION:*

- Make desires and values *work together —*
  not against each other!
- Enhance success in Health, Wealth and Romance —
  while maintaining compassionate ethical standards!
- Practical solutions to addressing social issues, human rights
  and broad-based prosperity
- Enjoy cheerful, compassionate feelings of goodwill towards
  others — *without getting taken advantage of!*

Extro • Dynamics™ is a well-rounded, balanced lifestyle
that really works!

Douglas Dunn

Word Wizards® ESCONDIDO, CALIFORNIA

Printed in the United States of America

Published by

Word Wizards®

Communications Excellence since 1972

P.O. Box 300721

Escondido, California 92030-0721 USA

760/781-1227

Internet: http://www.wordwiz72.com/exdyn.html

Library of Congress Cataloging-in-Publication Data:

Dunn, Douglas, 1950-
 Extro-dynamics : introspection, neutraspection, extrospection, action /
 Douglas Dunn.
      p.   cm.
 Includes bibliographical references and index.
 ISBN 978-0-944363-14-0 (pbk.)
   1. Conduct of life. 2. Caring. 3. Values. 4. Success.
 5. Happiness. I. Title.
 BJ1581.2.D79   1994
 170'.44--dc20   94-11592
                                                          CIP

Extro • Dynamics™ is a trademark of Douglas Dunn for lectures, seminars and educational programs.

Also by Douglas Dunn:

Dazhan®: a model for *how to* implement effective personal values and relationship skills using a combination of fiction and non-fiction in a fantasy-adventure setting along with non-fiction commentary and analysis

Comments made prior to the original 1995 first edition:

Continue to use to the fullest your beautiful gift of writing ... and you will be spreading the fragrance of His Love and His Peace all around you and wherever your book is read.

— **Mother Teresa**, (1910-1997)
  Nobel Laureate — 1979 Peace Prize
  From a letter to the author dated October 5, 1991

Not since Norman Vincent Peale's landmark book, *The Power of Positive Thinking*, has an author more clearly and simply outlined the practical pathway to balanced living. Please listen to Doug Dunn. He is a powerful voice of reason in a world desperately in need of principled thinking.

— **Bob Basso, Ph.D.**
  Motivational Speaker and author of numerous books on
  business management and personal development,
  Los Angeles, California

So many of us today feel fearful, powerless and confused by the tremendous challenges that confront us from our out-of-control society. Doug Dunn gives us a roadmap through this minefield. There is more than one path that can lead us to happiness and fulfillment, but they all share common basic principles. Some of these key principles are to be found in Doug's "amazing four-step secret for having it all."

— **Harold Kutler**
  Executive Director — Brother Benno Foundation,
  Oceanside, California (Soup kitchen/homeless shelter)

After 22 years of consciously working on myself to be non-judgmental and to love others unconditionally, I think *Extro • Dynamics* has given me the tools and the steps to get closer to my goal.

— **Dixie Bales**
  Volunteer Coordinator — Brother Benno Foundation,
  Oceanside, California (Soup kitchen/homeless shelter)

A carefully-constructed, well-organized plan for self, community and world improvement. Based on the interplay of self and society ... a sense of balance. A move away from the human potential over-preoccupation with self, yet dealing with human potential as a way of contributing to the general good. A way of being part of the solution rather than part of the problem. This is a hopeful book.

— **Rev. Carol Hilton**
  Palomar Unitarian Universalist Fellowship,
  Vista, California

CONTENTS

Acknowledgments

"We stand on the shoulders of those who go before us." Anyone who writes about implementing normative values necessarily draws from the many others, past and present, who have compiled a wealth of information and resources in psychology, the social sciences, religion, self-help programs and the popular media that is part of our multicultural heritage. While many of the experiences and observations in this book are entirely my own, including the specific way in which I have addressed seemingly unrelated issues through this unique four-step program, this work could not have been written without the earlier insights that so many others have provided.

I salute the philosophers, scientists, psychologists, counselors, religious leaders, mystics and social scientists from ancient times to the modern era, in all parts of the world, who have laid foundations of spirit and mind and heart that have inspired me to explore new directions. Many are acknowledged specifically at appropriate points throughout the book. Others have contributed to a general background of knowledge and culture that is less specifically identifiable. All are deeply appreciated. It is my hope that this work, too, will provide seed ideas from which others will go even further in offering practical guidelines to bring people together.

Special thanks to my wife, Thelma, and my daughter, JoAnn, for encouragement, support and specific ideas and suggestions for improving the presentation of this message. These two wonderful women, in very different ways, have provided me with excellent examples for success in implementing these values. Appreciation also to my son Tracy and daughter Darby in the Philippines, for their years of inspiration and closeness and desire to model these values in their own lives. I am also especially appreciative of the close relationship with my granddaughters Carina and Ella (daughters of JoAnn) and the opportunity she affords to share all that which is closest to me with yet another generation. Appreciation also to JoAnn's amazing husband, Shawnn, who has contributed so much to all of us since becoming a part of our family.

Special appreciation also to my twin brother, Dennis, for many years of encouragement and support, and for playing "devil's advocate" to challenge and test these ideas and concepts. My brother, Lowell, and sister, Karen also provided valuable feedback in the development of these values and techniques.

A special word of thanks, also, to my family in the Philippines, especially to my sister Marilyn Mantos and my brother Atty. Dionisio Mantos and the many others who have worked so hard with them in sharing this message overseas. Their tremendous efforts and enthusiasm have truly helped to make this an international project.

Special appreciation must also be expressed to my friends Leone Stein and Bob Basso for their encouragement, support and suggestions for editorial revisions to improve the clarity and readability of my efforts, utilizing their professional expertise in publishing and communications.

Finally, the most special acknowledgment must be expressed to *you*, the reader, through whose consciousness these little spots of ink on paper are made meaningful as thoughts and ideas.

Introduction

Making money? Success in love and romance? Health and longevity? Solving social and economic problems? Achieving meaningful personal values and personal satisfaction?

That's a tall order for one small book.

If it seems that we're trying to tackle too many different subjects at once, keep in mind that we're looking at the big picture. We're looking at the ways our desires, goals and values are interconnected. While many believe that personal success and ethical values are in conflict with each other, at great cost to themselves and to society, we will show how practical values of compassionate goodwill can enhance rather than detract from other goals.

And then there is the interplay between our individual lives and our roles as social beings. Some species of creatures are solitary — they hunt or forage and live mostly as individuals or in mating pairs. Other species are highly social, and hunt or forage in flocks, herds or packs. Human beings are all of the above.

Human beings are complex individuals, with multiple goals, desires and values that sometimes seem to pull in differing directions. But we are not just individuals. We are also members of social groups — families, communities and nations. We have many elements that need to be integrated and balanced in order to achieve deep personal satisfaction, contentment and the real peace of true, lasting happiness.

Have you ever noticed how some people work very hard to try to pull together all the different elements in their lives? They want to enjoy successful careers, raise their kids with good skills and values, enjoy hobbies and special interests, participate in community affairs, develop healthy lifestyle habits with an exercise program and good dietary habits, find love and romance that doesn't go stale, and still find some time to relax and just enjoy some semblance of a social life, all while trying to conform with the moral and ethical values they believe in. They frantically try to juggle their schedules or find shortcuts to success in an increasing frustrating and futile attempt to "do it all." Other people just say, "Why bother?" and just give up.

To those who try the hardest to find romantic love, or financial security, or health, or to live a lifestyle of compassion and goodwill for your fellow humans, I would ask, have you found success in your goals? Are you rich? Are you satisfied in romance? Have you found health and physical well-being? Are you compassionate? *Have you found what you are looking for?*

We force our goals and desires to compete against each other, instead of reinforcing each other. It's tough out there! In the hectic pace of daily survival, we spend so much effort trying to achieve health, wealth and love that we just don't have time for "compassion" or "values."

Yet some people *are successful* in blending the seemingly unrelated demands in their lives into a balanced and harmonious lifestyle. Ironically, these are the people who seem to glide through life with little effort, attracting money, possessions, romance or good health as if they had a special magnet. How do they *achieve more* with *less effort? Why is it so easy for some people, while most of us struggle so hard, with so little to show for our efforts?*

Those who learn to attract success easily are often not conscious of what that they do that makes them so successful. Somewhere along the line they picked up the attributes of success, which they follow without conscious effort. Some people grew up with "natural gifts" of business acumen or romantic prowess or a natural tendency toward good health. Others, who feel deep compassion, grew up in nurturing, loving environments where they naturally acquired the joyful feelings of compassion. If you ask them what they do that's different than the rest of us, they will often shrug their shoulders and say they "just grew up that way."

So what about the rest of us? If we didn't "just grow up that way," then is there no hope for us?

Practical skills and values

We want to examine the ways in which successful people are able to link important goals, so that effort in one area promotes success in all areas, instead of trying to make each area work separately and often with contradictory and frustrating results. We need to be able to "push one button" that does several things at once. We can only do this if our goals, desires and successful implementation of the highest possible real values are aligned in a practical balance that brings harmony to these separate areas of our lives and allows us to manage them with greater ease.

The *power of practical compassion in **action*** is more than just a "feel good" message of love and peace. It is love, and it is peace and it does bring contentment, joy and happiness — good feelings. But it is so much more. It is the power of direct but compassionate *action* by which Gandhi brought down the British Empire, the greatest empire the world had ever known. It was how Martin Luther King Jr. and Nelson Mandela brought down centuries-old systems of institutionalized racial injustice. And it was how the families and survivors of the massacre at Mother Emanuel AME Church in Charleston, South Carolina, brought down a symbol of hate that others had tried to lower for 54 years, by repaying hatred and violence with love and forgiveness that softened long-hardened hearts. This same power can improve every aspect of our personal, social and productive lives. The *power of practical compassion in **action*** not only brings personal contentment, happiness, joy and serenity, it also makes our lives better and more successful as it brings goals, values and desires into harmony with each other instead of working against each other.

And the same principle of *practical compassion in **action*** that, at the level of public policy, can bring down empires and undo centuries of institutionalized oppression can also, at the level of individual private lives, reverse negative energy, heal emotional suffering, create a harmonious environment of compassionate joy, and bring values and goals into harmony with success objectives.

This book provides an underlying foundation of *practical* skills and values, with specific examples for applying them to our wide range of needs and desires. You CAN *have it all!* And it's *easier than you think!*

Using Extro • Dynamics™

The first half of this book is organized into three sections:

1. Underlying concepts — *why* Extro • Dynamics works the way it does — letting our desires and values reinforce each other and work together instead of against each other;

2. Specific guidelines to interpersonal interactions — *what* Extro • Dynamics is;

3. Implementing Extro • Dynamics in *your* lifestyle — *how* to make it work in a variety of situations and interactions.

Three additional sections show how to apply these lifestyle guidelines to the issues and problems that affect our daily lives:

1. **Personal issues**: using Extro • Dynamics to enhance your opportunities for achieving personal goals of financial success, romantic love and a long and healthy life.

2. **Public policy issues**: applying Extro • Dynamics to community issues, to prevent and solve social and economic problems. Families, communities and nations are made up of individuals, and the same principles that work at an individual level can be adapted an applied at levels of social interaction.

3. **How to teach** *practical* values of compassionate, joyful success to others — both children and adults.

By understanding the practical skills and values of Extro • Dynamics, **you can achieve personal happiness and contentment, and improve your prospects for success in personal and community goals.** This book shows you how to do it — how to bring the different parts of your life together in harmonious balance.

Material is Progressive — *Read in Sequence!*

In using this book, you may find it tempting to skip past the underlying material in the early chapters because you are eager to read about techniques for increasing health, wealth or romance. Please note that the material in this book is sequentially progressive, and that those later chapters refer to basic skills and techniques presented earlier. If you have not mastered preliminary information, then it will not be possible to understand or implement more advanced techniques.

This book is *not* a "how to" book for making money, a handbook for improving romantic techniques or a manual of physical fitness. This book does touch on each of those subjects, and offers very specific suggestions for how to bring practical implementation of the highest values into harmony with these desires for improvement in each of these areas, the real point of this book *is* to present a balanced lifestyle program based on practical values of compassionate goodwill in a practical, realistic way, and show how these values contribute to achieving success in other areas instead of working against them as so many people tragically believe.

More important, it is not just about pretending to have these values or mastering the appearance of these values. It is about how to actually cultivate feelings of universal compassion and goodwill even when — *especially when!* — you don't feel like it. This book presents realistic strategies for living by practical values in real-life situations, even difficult situations. Others have found these techniques to be valuable in daily interactions, social situations, interpersonal interactions in the work place and, yes, even under challenging conditions. Often such techniques can prevent difficult situations or provide the means for healing from them, for yourself and for those who make them difficult.

Let us travel the path of understanding *practical* skills and values that link the many dimensions of our potentials for enjoying personal success, and how these factors can work in harmony to reinforce each other rather than compete for our limited energy resources. Let us go beyond theories and ideas to develop a specific lifestyle model that will work in *your* daily pattern of interpersonal interactions.

To Be Happy

*Financial security, romantic love and a long, healthy life are spe-
cific forms of the same common denominator — the desire to be
happy.*

*In our search for the underlying links that join these goals that
seem to be separate, we must first understand the nature of happiness and how human beings achieve it. We can then apply our
general findings to specific secondary goals, such as health,
wealth and love in a program of lifestyle guidelines that will
enable us to achieve these forms of happiness, as well as many
others beyond what we have even imagined.*

Seek and You Might *Not* Find

In the movie *Man Friday,* about Robinson Crusoe, with Richard Roundtree and Peter O'Toole, the "civilized" Crusoe (O'Toole) is determined to teach proper culture to the primitive savage, Friday (Roundtree). Crusoe decides to teach the value of competition by running a "race" to "see who is the *winner.*"

"Winner?" responds Friday with a puzzled expression.

"The best runner," answers Crusoe.

"The fastest runner?"

"The important thing is not whether you win or lose ... The important thing is *how* you play. The important thing is *how* you run."

Crusoe gives the signal and the race is on!

Crusoe strains with full determination, reaching deep into his aging body for every ounce of strength and speed he can muster. He runs hard, sweating and breathing with deep, heaving sighs.

Friday, young and strong, runs with high-stepping, graceful pleasure — not as fast, but a celebration of physical joy.

Gasping for breath, Crusoe stumbles across the finish line first and collapses on the sandy beach. Friday follows joyously, squatting alongside the Englishman.

Crusoe responds with angry disgust. "You *let* me win! You weren't *trying!*"

"You won?" Friday is shocked!

"I got here first."

"But you said 'the important thing is *how* you run.' I ran very beautifully. I enjoyed every step along the sand. You did not seem to enjoy the running. Your body was jerking and unhappy."

Crusoe decides that perhaps Friday is too primitive to grasp such advanced notions as "competition." "Forget what I said before," he scowls. "The important thing is to *win!"*

As members of the human race, each of us wants to *win!* Like Robinson Crusoe, however, we often are not sure exactly what that means. On the road to becoming "winners," we encounter many paradoxes and seeming contradictions.

Friday is able to enjoy the energy of his body in motion, surrounded by a beautiful, natural setting. Crusoe wins his race. But, in considering his pain and exhaustion we might ask, "What, exactly, did he win?"

Humans want to enjoy financial security, romantic love and a long and healthy life. We want to be happy! It is normal and desirable that we should try to make our experiences pleasant.

Many who work very hard to find happiness never gain the riches, romance, or physical well-being they seek. Such people come to believe that "if you don't take care of your own self first, no one else is going to do it for you." The more they stumble, the more they exert themselves. The emphasis is on "me, me, me" and to Hell with anyone else. They would suggest that we treat the people around us nicely and pleasantly *if it's to our advantage to do so,* and ruthlessly and cruelly if *that* is most advantageous. Their operative slogans are, "Looking out for #1" and "Winning Through Intimidation," titles of books written by Robert Ringer in the 1970's that set the tone for the "me-first" 1980's [Ringer, 1973 and 1977].

What is the legacy of this rampant "me-first"-ism? What I see in looking around the world is:

1. Increased willingness to be openly selfish, disregarding the needs and feelings of other people.

2. An increase in crime, especially crimes of violence.

3. Increased fear, and increased individual alienation.

4. A decrease in personal concern and the quality of service provided by craftsmen. Do you call your TV repair person, auto repair person, plumber, lawyer, or insurance agent with complete confidence that they *really care* about earning an honest day's pay in return for *solving your problem?* While there are many refreshing exceptions, too often they want to charge as much as they can for doing as little as possible.

5. An over-all retreat from concern with the general welfare of other people, or in trying to improve society as a whole.

For all our efforts in trying to *make ourselves happy,* I would ask **are we happy?**

Is life in our greedy, "get rich quick," twentieth-century technocracy really any more pleasant or happy than, say, in pre-Western Samoa or Hawaii?

With all our "labor-saving" gadgets, most of us are working harder than ever, while a small leisure class is bored silly and still can't always find the key to real happiness.

We have developed more fantastic inventions; we can perform more unbelievable miracles; we can think more profound thoughts and discuss more involved questions than the great minds of yesteryear would have dreamed about even in fantasy. We have also developed more fantastic problems, performed more unbelievable destruction, and ended up with more ulcers, headaches, and tension than the most sadistic minds of old could have imagined.

What went wrong? Where is the fallacy in saying that if you want to be happy, go make yourself happy?

By the time the 1990's rolled around, even Robert Ringer, the "#1 Intimidator," had recognized the failure of pure greed to produce happiness. His latest writings included such topics as morality, interpersonal relations skills and even a discussion of the importance of compassion for others [Ringer, 1990].

We have all seen many examples of those who lead shallow, empty lives despite great financial wealth or fame or glamour — such as Leona Helmsley, Zsa Zsa Gabor, Jim and Tammy Bakker,

17

Ferdinand and Imelda Marcos, and many other real-life examples — that it has almost become a cliché that wealth is a cause of misery (rather than a valued resource squandered by those who do not understand the real nature and origin of happiness). Such people seem to have everything, yet suffer lives of painful unhappiness, stress, tension, escape from reality, and sometimes even suicide.

In the movie *Wall Street,* the character played by Michael Douglas boldly states that, "Greed is good ... greed works!" Of course, he ends up in jail (followed soon afterward in real-life by Wall-Streeters Ivan Boesky, Michael Milken and Charles Keating under amazingly similar conditions). They are wrong. Greed is not good; it doesn't work — and we're going to show you *why* it doesn't work, along with a clear alternative that *does.*

On the other hand, there are also those who are very poor or who willingly sacrifice great wealth yet still find great happiness and contentment. Since there are also happy rich people, and miserable poor people, material wealth does not seem to be the determining factor.

The Failure of Selfishness

A "me-first" strategy doesn't understand the *nature* of happiness. If we want to go out and get something, we should at least know what it is!

Matter and Energy — Two Dimensions: To understand happiness (and how to get it) we must understand how the different elements of our world interact.

Planet Earth is just a great big rock, whirling through space. By itself, it is hard and cold and lifeless. It is made up of sand and water and chemicals of many kinds. The rocks, elements, and molecules of Earth and beyond represent a dimension of **things**; of *matter*. This physical dimension exists independently — with no wants, no needs, and no feelings.

If I take a rock and smash it into a thousand pieces, it doesn't care. It has no fear or pain, because it has no feelings. It has no consciousness or awareness, even of its own existence. It's just there. It's just a thing.

Physical objects exist unchangingly, unless acted upon by some external force. They initiate no activity of their own. If I set the rock on my desk, *and nothing acts to change it or move it,* how long will it stay there? Forever! It doesn't need food, water or air. As external forces such as heat or erosion act upon it, its form or position may change, but the *matter* — the *thing itself* — will remain indefinitely. It does not need nor want nor feel any thing.

Physical objects are tangible in nature. You can chase, catch, touch and hold them. You can put them under a microscope and examine them, or use instruments to measure them.

But there is another dimension in nature. There are little pockets of feeling and thought within the minds of conscious beings, which break up the emptiness of the physical dimension. This is the dimension of **consciousness**; of mental and emotional *energy*. This is a dimension of feeling and awareness.[1]

Consciousness is *not* physical. You *can't* just reach out and grab some for yourself, or chase it like a baseball or Frisbee. You can't hold it or measure it like a tangible object. As Nathaniel Hawthorne is quoted as saying: "Happiness is like a butterfly which, when pursued, is just beyond your grasp, but, if you will sit down quietly, may alight upon you."

While the direct pursuit of one's own happiness may be counterproductive, this does not mean that we cannot set in motion the conditions out of which it naturally arises — if we understand them. Thus it is our goal to understand not merely what happiness is *not,* but more importantly what it is and what conditions lead to it, and how happiness and values can be made to work together.

Unlike physical matter, the energy of consciousness is not static. If I take a four-year-old child, active and restless, and tell her to sit in the corner, and leave her unsupervised, how long will she stay there? Ooops! There she goes! Why does she run off? She

---

[1]It is not claimed here that "consciousness" is unique to humans. It is almost certain that animals such as monkeys, apes, dolphins, dogs and cats have some form of consciousness. It may also be true of birds, other mammals and "lower" vertebrates. What about insects? Plants? One-celled animals? To whatever extent animal consciousness exists, the same principles would apply; however, I do not presume to determine the cut-off point, focusing only on *human* consciousness.

gets *bored!* Unlike the rock, the *energy* of consciousness *does* have feelings and desires and *does* initiate spontaneous activity. It never stops. Even in sleep, the mind remains active. If consciousness stops, it dies. Feelings — *E-motion* — are "**E**nergy" in "**motion**."

Another characteristic of consciousness is that it does not exist independently. If I chain the little girl to the corner so she *can't* run away, and leave her there with no food or water, how long would she stay there? Just thinking about it is awful, because it is so contrary to the nature of consciousness. But it wouldn't be harmful or cruel to a *rock.* Consciousness *does* depend on the surrounding environment for the sustenance of its physical needs.[1]

To summarize the distinctions between physical objects and processes of consciousness or feelings:

Objects / Things	Feelings / Consciousness
• Physical / Tangible (matter) [can chase + catch]	• Process of energy / not tangible [can't hold or touch]
• Exists independently	• Depends on environment to exist
• Inactive — "remains at rest"	
• No feelings or awareness	• Active, ongoing — if stops, dies
	• **All** Feelings/Awareness/Consc.

If you look out at the world, you can see how these two dimensions fit together:

Wherever you are, look around. Visualize consciousness as being represented by light, and matter as being represented by darkness. Wherever you see buildings, furniture, or cement, imagine a dark "nothing" (no feelings or consciousness). Wherever

---

[1] This characterization of the difference between matter and consciousness might be construed as being in conflict with the excellent technical and theoretical discussion of consciousness by Daniel C. Dennett, in his 1991 book, *Consciousness Explained.* Dennett argues against concepts of "dualism" (as proposed by the French philosopher Renes Decartes — "I think, therefore I am") that separate the experience of consciousness from the biology of a *physical* brain (pp. 33-39; 106). Extro • Dynamics does not seek to analyze matter or consciousness literally in terms of physics or biology. Even Dennett acknowledges that, for practical purposes, human beings perceive a *functional* distinction between the physical brain and the process of consciousness which would apply whether a true dualism exists or if the mind-body difference is merely a functional perception (pp. 126-138); it is this day-to-day reality of perception which is addressed here.

you see cars or trees, imagine a dark nothing. If you see the sun, or illuminated light bulbs, still imagine them as empty dark spots, to represent their lack of consciousness.

By now, most of the surrounding view should have gone dark. However, floating within the darkness, wherever you see the minds of Living Beings, are scattered little dots of light. Only within the minds of sentient beings does "meaning" or "awareness" exist.

As you can see, these little pockets of feeling and experience are sparsely scattered, and are only a small part of the universe. Even if you are at a crowded stadium watching a football game, the thousands of spectators in the crowd are dwarfed by the huge structure of granite, steel, glass and lights, as well as the surrounding earth and its atmosphere.

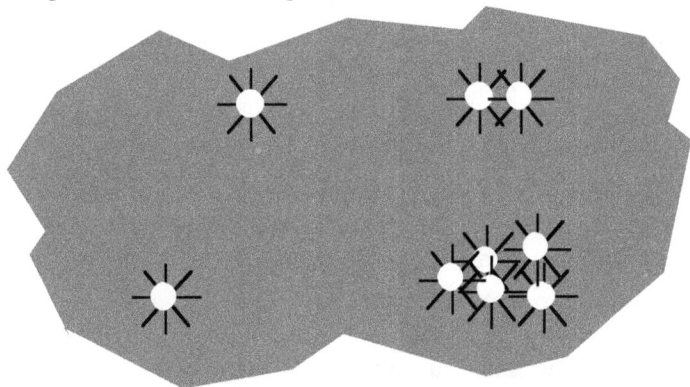

The vast, non-feeling dimension of Physical Objects encompasses the little "lights" of Consciousness, which exist within the surrounding environment.

The dimension of consciousness has developed tools for operating within a surrounding physical environment that is neither hospitable nor hostile. The "mind" doesn't just float around in space by itself. Consciousness is housed in a physical shell, a body, physical in nature, but controlled by consciousness. This body has sense organs that gather information from the environment and transmit it to the mind where it is processed as non-physical perceptions of experience to be interpreted and evaluated. This body also has arms and legs and other goodies, capable of acting upon the physical environment to do what it wants.

The dimension of consciousness must operate within its surrounding physical dimension, on which it depends for stimulation and sustenance. Consciousness is an active, ongoing *process*. It is energy. It is in motion. A Living Being *must interact with its environment.*

The environment, however, doesn't care. It won't come to the consciousness for interaction or to offer sustenance. In order to enjoy this interaction, the consciousness must **go to the environment** — it must **reach <u>away</u> from itself** to find the stimulation and sustenance that it needs.

This happiness we seek is within that dimension of *energy* — a *process of emotion.* It doesn't operate like a *physical object.* The big mistake the "me-firsters" make is in trying to chase and catch happiness directly, the same as they would go out and "get" a thing or object.

In trying to "make themselves happy," the "me-firsters" make two important mistakes in failing to recognize that:

1. Happiness is an active process of energy, not a static object. You can't just reach out and grab it or catch it *by direct pursuit* like a baseball or a Frisbee.

2. The consciousness must reach *away* from itself, into the surrounding environment on which it depends for stimulation and sustenance. When people focus *toward* themselves, trying to make themselves happy, their attention is in exactly the wrong direction.

Our desire for happiness can only be fulfilled through the *process* that results from the interaction between the separate elements of matter (objects and things) and energy (as feelings or consciousness).

We need to *reach away from self.* When our primary focus of attention is towards our own selves — as the "me-firsters" would have us do — we are headed in the wrong direction. The more we try to make ourselves happy by direct pursuit, the more we deny the very process of consciousness that requires us to *interact with the surrounding environment.*

Some attention to care of one's self is necessary, and there is some happiness in a reflective enjoyment of Self. But a *predominance* of self-preoccupation causes pressure, tension, and frustration instead of happiness.

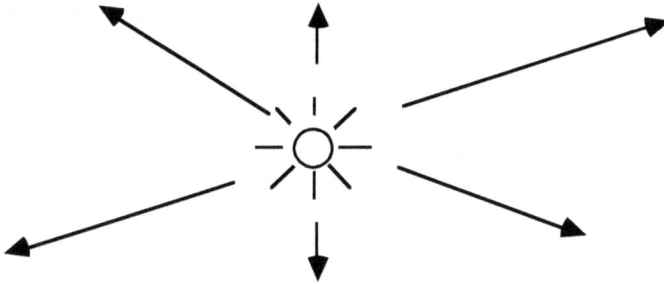

Little "lights" of consciousness must reach out to the surrounding environment to find the stimulation and sustenance they need

All unhappiness can be traced to direct preoccupation with one's own Self, whether voluntary or not. For example: Physical pain causes unhappiness because it forces attention to the Self; Worry, fear, or over-sensitivity to petty criticism are all unpleasant feelings rooted in self-directed concern.

In the movie *Hook,* Peter Banning (the grown-up Peter Pan), played by Robin Williams, was a successful lawyer who had achieved great wealth. But he could not find contentment and real happiness until he tossed away his mobile phone and reached beyond himself to embrace the people and adventures from the surrounding environment.

The Rolling Stones sang, "I can't get no satisfaction ... but I try." perhaps that line should be changed to, "I can't get no satisfaction ... *because* I try."

Legendary naturist John Muir lived simply, hiking through the mountains of his beloved Yosemite Valley. Muir addressed in his own down-to-earth way, the paradox of trying to satisfy oneself with material riches, by comparing himself to one of the well-known wealthy railroad tycoons of his era. As recounted in the editor's introduction to his book, "During the Harriman Expedition to Alaska in 1899, someone mentioned the great wealth of the sponsor, the railroad magnate E. H. Harriman. Muir replied,

'Why, I am richer than Harriman. I have all the money I want and he hasn't.' " [Muir, editor's introduction, p. xvi].

As we will show later in more detail, this is not to negate or deny the importance of self, or to focus our energies in an exclusively "outward" direction. Reaching "away from self-preoccupation" is not a denial of self, but blending and sharing the experience of self with the stimulation and resources that it needs from the surrounding environment. In reality, an obsession with self distorts true self interest needs.

Consciousness is a *process*. Happiness is a journey, not a destination. Some people may think, "When I get a new (car / house / job) then I'll be happy." But when they get it, the novelty soon wears off and becomes routine. To be happy, they must keep *active* and move on to the next thing. People with a lot of money who seek this direct pursuit of happiness become frustrated with their inability to keep up with the insatiability of a self-directed focus. There is never enough to satisfy the continuous gulf between expectation and disillusionment.

The Paradox of Happiness

This is the "Paradox of Happiness": Those who try hardest to make themselves happy are the least successful, while happiness seems to fall almost accidentally on those who are too involved with other things to worry about it.

The late Dr. Leo Buscaglia, long-time professor of education at the University of Southern California, who for many years taught an innovative course on "Love," has written enthusiastically about the joy of living. He relates a story about this phenomenon that occurred when he was a teenager. Two weeks before Christmas the largest present he had ever seen was put under the Christmas tree, with *his* name on it! For two weeks, his mind ran wild with imaginings far beyond reality, trying to envision what could be inside such a box. Finally Christmas came, and the moment he had been anticipating arrived. He writes, "Even as I was opening it, I remember experiencing a vague sense of disappointment — the Great Mystery was about to end and I would no longer be able to engage in my soaring dreams." The gift was a beautiful handmade desk from his Uncle Louie — a truly lovely and much-needed gift. "But by this time nothing of this world could have satisfied my expectations. I can't imagine what I had expected. Still, in that disappointment was a lesson that would last a lifetime." [Buscaglia, 1986] It is ironic that, for many people, Christmas — which is supposed to be the happiest time of the year — is filled with the greatest sadness and disappointments, because the heightened expectations of self-preoccupation lead to disillusionment.

The paradox in our experience of happiness is similar to the paradox in how we perceive the passing of time: when we are inactive or bored, time seems to pass slowly, and intervals of time seem long; but, in looking back later, these intervals seem short because they provide few memories (little activity). On the other hand, when we are busy and active, the actual passage of time seems to move quickly; but, when we look back later, seems long — filled with many memories (much activity). It only seems contradictory or paradoxical if we look at it as though it were a *physical object* rather than the *process of energy* that it really is.

Resolution of this "paradox" comes from reversing the self-directed focus, using natural processes of consciousness that are capable of flowing *away from self* — seeking happiness as a process of energy rather than as an object or thing.

This is not to say that we remain focused in an "outward" perspective, or that we live our lives directed externally. All consciousness must still be experienced within the self. It is a process of *interaction.* Sources of stimulation or sustenance are found outside, but are brought from the outside to within the consciousness, where experience actually occurs.

This can be compared to the way a television set works:

You can go out and buy the finest, most expensive, most technologically advanced TV available, and bring it home and set it up in your living room. You can look at the set, and the fine craftsmanship of the cabinet, and appreciate the technological wonder it represents.

But admiring the set is not why we buy a TV. The real use of a TV is to *turn it on* and set in motion a *process* of electrical *energy.*

Colors, sounds, and images appear on the screen! Where do they come from? If you take the top or sides off the box, you don't see little people running around inside, singing, dancing, or having adventures in faraway lands. The scenes, people and actions are brought from all around the world, from *outside the TV,* and crystallized into focus within the little mechanical box!

The TV is driven by electricity. The flow of electrons, like the flow of consciousness, is *energy,* requiring a continuous, active power source. If the energy stops, so does the TV. The stimulation that the TV "seeks" is the compilation of signals, encoded with information or entertainment, originating from outside the set, whether from a transmitter far away or the videotape of a nearby VCR.

But what if you push the "on" button and nothing happens? Before a TV set can begin to operate, it must be in good mechanical repair. It must be well maintained. Thus, as a pre-requisite to any real use of the set, certain attention must be given to the set itself.

In much the same way, the individual Self is valuable for its own sake, and affords some extent of pleasure in its own right: reflective or introspective feelings, pride in achievement, or pleasant memories. Similarly, in developing positive experiences (happiness) within the Self, certain *individual* needs must be taken care of. A good self-attitude is important; an understanding of one's self lets a person experience and understand the inherent value represented in their own consciousness; skills and talents should be developed, so that no matter what "channel" the "set" is tuned to, the individual can function effectively — with *genuine* self-esteem[1]. But the active, ongoing process of consciousness cannot be maximized in that kind of activity alone. Self-preoccupation,

---

[1]Some have ridiculed the idea of "self-esteem," seeking to portray it as a simplistic "feel-good" diversion from serious issues. Serious researchers universally agree that genuine self-esteem is essential for the development of other skills and values, but must be differentiated from flattery, its cheap, frivolous impostor whose phoniness is easily recognized and makes others feel degraded, if that is all they are worth. In contrast, authentic self-esteem is rooted in cultivating, recognizing and celebrating legitimate talents, achievements and admirable qualities that are known to be valid. Genuine self-esteem, built on real abilities and real achievements, resonates in the soul and forms the foundation on which to expand our best attributes.

without interaction with the processes of energy from beyond the self, is like buying a beautiful TV, and just staring for hours at the blank screen, stubbornly refusing to turn it on.

But which direction is "away from self"? If we can't reach out physically and touch a non-tangible commodity such as happiness, which direction do we go? Which channel do you watch on TV? All of them, of course! There are many choices: the whole environment. The key is to enjoy the active process by which the consciousness interacts with all that surrounds it: becoming "lost" in a pleasant or interesting activity; feeling the excitement of thrilling discoveries, or of inventiveness, or of creativity; enjoying moments of spontaneous playfulness; enjoying the absorbed interests of a special hobby or project — and any other diversion that leads a person's concerns away from the Self. There is no limit to the many ways in which the consciousness can enjoy happiness by reaching away from self. In fact, enjoyment of many interests or activities may generate a more complete, versatile exploration of unselfishly-directed experiences.

This is a fundamental truth, long known to the greatest teachers of value, from religion, philosophy, and the social sciences.

A variation of this concept — that all suffering is caused by *desire*, and the inability of human beings to satisfy the desires of self-preoccupation — was the essence of Gautama Buddha's "enlightenment," and the foundation of his "four noble truths," which became the main pillar of Buddhist religious thought. [Bukkyo Dendo Kyokai, pp. 38-39; Burtt p. 30] Blended with the Hindu concepts from Gautama's upbringing, these ideas helped to shape much of Eastern philosophy. The philosophy of Taoism, developed by Lao Tse in China about the same time, similarly teaches that desire leads to frustration or unhappiness [Lao Tse, p. 27].

The Dalai Lama, a secular leader of the Tibetan nation and spiritual leader of Tibetan Buddhists, writes about this paradox, "I believe that suffering is caused by ignorance, and that people inflict pain on others in pursuit of their own happiness or satisfaction. Yet true happiness comes ... through cultivation of altruism, of love, of compassion...." [Dalai Lama, p. 270]

Christianity is based on the paradox that "he who would be greatest among you is the least of all," "the first shall be last," "he who loses his soul shall find it," and of course, an ensuing doctrine based on universal compassion.

Mother Teresa, winner of the 1979 Nobel Peace Prize and founder of the Missionaries of Charity in Calcutta, India, and other troubled areas around the world, echoes the same message. Living a simple life without luxuries, she does not seek happiness; on the contrary, she seeks hardship and sacrifice. She says, "We have very little, so we have nothing to be preoccupied with. The more you have, the more you are occupied .... the less you have, the more free you are .... We are perfectly happy .... The rich ... are never satisfied." [Desmond, pp. 11-14]

In modern times, the English philosopher and mathematician Bertrand Russell was well known for his joyful spontaneity, which he enjoyed until his death at the age of 97. He characterized the evolution of happiness in his life this way: "I was not born happy. As a child, my favorite hymn was 'Weary of earth and laden with my sin.' ... In adolescence, I hated life and was continually on the verge of suicide.... Now, on the contrary, I enjoy life; I might almost say that with every year that passes I enjoy it more ... due to a diminishing preoccupation with myself." [Russell, page 5-7. (See also page 176)]

Similarly, one of the key tools of Alcoholics Anonymous and other self-help groups for overcoming various forms of addiction, is to seek an escape from "self-obsession." Once a person is able to break free of self-preoccupation, it becomes possible to overcome the enslaving power of compulsive behaviors. The same tools can be as useful in everyday situations as in overcoming illness.

It is easy to visualize how this process operates. If you imagine a person who is discouraged, depressed, or otherwise not happy (as a result of tensions at work, or problems with romance, or whatever), the person may experience an initial resistance to any kind of activity. If the person can overcome this resistance and *do something,* the despondency, pressure, or other (self-directed) symptoms of unhappiness will subside while the person is directed towards other involvements. Or consider the way a self-preoccupied person might think about an unpleasant chore. As long as they look toward self, they dread the task, putting it off and brooding over it. But if they can channel that energy into the environment, they can just do the chore and get it over with. If they really get caught up in it, they might even find a way to make it fun! In the words of advice columnist Ann Landers, "Happiness is what happens when you get too busy to be miserable." [Column dated 8-10-94]

Dr. Leo F. Buscaglia, who has traveled extensively, relates the story of a man stuck in an airport because his flight was delayed by a blizzard. The man was ranting and raving and screaming that he *had to* get out of the airport, even though it was impossible. Another woman there handled the situation differently. She chose to gather together all the children and keep them occupied so their frazzled parents could go off to enjoy something to eat. She was able to find meaning and enjoyment despite the delay. Dr. Buscaglia relates that, following his telling of this experience, others have written him to share the innovative ways in which they have responded to the same situation (not unusual in the world of air travel), and how it has affected their attitudes while traveling. [Buscaglia 1982, pp. 198-199]

From the surrounding environment we encounter interactions that are joyous and uplifting, as well as those that bring danger or harm. As we reach into the environment, and draw its value from the external to within the self, we must focus on that which is positive and avoid dwelling on that which is negative. By choosing the direction of our focus, we can choose happiness.

Yet the process involves much more than merely deciding to think happy thoughts. As we interact with our environment, we cannot avoid stumbling across that which is hurtful or destructive.

We need to understand *skills and techniques* for reaching into the environment and choosing positive experiences, while simultaneously avoiding that which is negative, with tools for coping with the negative when unavoidable and converting negative experiences into the positive benefits we desire. This will be an important part of Extro • Dynamics™.

There are *many* choices! Extro • Dynamics™ is just one approach for reaching away from self to set in motion the process of a happy lifestyle. There are also many other valuable tools, offered by others who have contributed to the development of human potential, from the fields of psychology, philosophy, religion, social sciences, and self-help groups. This program (or any program) should not be thought of as *"the"* answer, but *"an"* answer. All available tools should be used together, reinforcing each other where appropriate or individually as dictated by circumstances, toward the common goal of improving the quality of our lives.

Chapter 1 Summary:
We cannot find happiness (as health, wealth or love — or any other form) by just trying to make ourselves happy. We can't chase or catch intangible processes of energy in the same way as physical objects. We need to reach *away from self preoccupation* in positive directions that set in motion *happy* processes of consciousness.

2

Desires & Values

What happens when our *desires* seem to conflict with our *values?* Is it wrong to want financial security? Health? Romantic love?

Many times we feel torn between the things we want and the values we wish to live by. Sometimes those who seem unable to live by their beliefs are not simply hypocrites. They may be sincerely struggling to accommodate the various demands that seem to be in conflict, expending valuable time and energy trying to swim against the current and make everything work. How can we make our values work *together,* reinforcing each other?

Universal Values
In Chapter 1 we saw that pursuit of the universal human desire (happiness) presents us with a paradox, and how this paradox is resolved through the interaction between the separate dimensions of matter (objects or things) and energy (as feelings or consciousness). At the same time, consistent, almost universal messages about ethical values also come from widely divergent sources:

Religion
Unselfish compassion is the stated centerpiece of Judeo-Christian ethics. It is also prominent in the Hindu, Sikh, Taoist, Bahá'í and Wiccan (and other Nature) religions, and also plays a central role in Buddhism [Bukkyo Dendo Kyokai.] The Qur'an (Koran), holy book of Islam, also stresses recurring themes of mercy, compassion, kindness, forgiveness and of almsgiving to those in need. [See Sûrah II:263; III:134; IV:36, 114; and XVI:90 and others.]

31

It is important to note, however, that while value systems that are both moral and practical should, ideally, be consistent with major belief systems that resonate with large numbers of people, our morals, values and ethics must also be able to stand alone, independent of religious beliefs. Non-believers are no less moral or ethical than believers. Belief systems should be in harmony with what is right, not the other way around. To say otherwise — to say that something is right "because God says so" — is to reduce ethics, morals and values to the ultimate in "might makes right."

Peer Group Influences

In the late 1960's, a similar message of "love," "peace" and "brotherhood" became popularized by social and media influences. A popular song by Jackie DeShannon told us to "Put a Little Love in Your Heart." Television, movies and the popular press emphasized the same social issues and values, but from a source that was not only non-religious, but often openly hostile to religion. New Age groups and non-religious movements claimed beliefs based on "love" and "peace."

Academic Disciplines

Today, similar values are also echoed from a wide range of academic disciplines, including philosophy, sociology, education and psychology, with teachings from Erich Fromm, Abraham Maslow, Karl Menninger, Leo Buscaglia and many others. Similar values also form the core on which a broad number of personal development organizations and self-help programs were established to help people confront and overcome the many personal and social challenges of modern life.

In the book *The Road Less Traveled,* psychiatrist M. Scott Peck clearly shows the interrelation between the science of psychology and spirituality (not necessarily religion belief in the supernatural).

Politics

Even in current American political trends, "compassion" is held up as a standard of value by both Democrats (with an agenda of "putting people first" to help those in need that was the basis of Bill Clinton's and Barack Obama's successful campaigns for President) and Republicans (who try to increase the efficiency of service to others through a "kinder, gentler" volunteerism from the "thousand points of light" espoused by George H.W. Bush or the claims of "compassionate conservatism" of his son, George W.), or the values-driven "bleeding-heart conservatism" of William Bennett and Jack Kemp).

With all the disagreement among science, religion, popular culture and political ideologies, if there is a common value they can all agree on, perhaps there is something to it! But why compassion?

The Origin of Values

Are our desires really in conflict with our values? Is it wrong to want both happiness *and* success? We need to understand the relationship between happiness and values, so we can develop specific strategies for achieving *both* our happiness *and* our good values, along with our specific desires for health, wealth and love.

We have seen that the universal common denominator among moral systems is compassion. But why is this so?

We also noted earlier that values must derive from their inherent relation to right and wrong, not because an all-powerful deity pronounces them so; otherwise, it is nothing more than a glorified version of "might makes right" — God has the most power, there— fore he or she or they make the rules.

In Chapter 1 we saw how the dimensions of physical matter and the energy of consciousness interact. Out of this interaction between consciousness and its surrounding environment emerges not only the process for achieving happiness, but also the origins of "value." "Value" is not another dimension, but rather a byproduct of the interaction between the consciousness and its environment.

By itself, the physical dimension has no meaning, awareness, or value. Yet we all have certain *things* that we hold dear, which are *valuable* to us. Some people might ascribe great value to a Rolls Royce or an expensive piece of art. Or very simple physical objects, such as a small gift, flowers, or mementos may be very meaningful. But the meaning or value is added to the object in how it is experienced *within the consciousness* of a sentient being as it interacts with external stimuli. The physical objects themselves have no meaning or value until they are experienced within sentient consciousness — and *evaluated*.

A rock, for example, just exists. It has no idea of value. It isn't a good rock. It isn't a bad rock. It's just a rock. If no one ever finds it or experiences it in some way then it will just stay there. Now, suppose some people are walking along and see the rock. If they just see it and pass by and forget about it, then it probably had very little real effect, and still remains essentially meaningless. But if one of them stumbles over it and gets hurt, then the rock has had a little greater influence, and they perceive it as a negative experience. It is a "bad" rock. But then if they pick it up, and discover that it is a diamond, they may get very happy about this newfound treasure, and so it is a positive experience, outweighing the small pain, and it becomes a "good" rock. If the people then begin fighting over who gets to keep the diamond, and in their struggle several of them get hurt and the diamond gets lost, then it really didn't do them any good, and still ends up as a "bad" rock.

By itself, though, it was just a rock. Just like fire: by itself it is neither good nor bad. But when it touches our experience, we make it "good" or "bad," depending on whether it cooks our food or burns our house down. Similarly, the value of the Rolls Royce is in the experience of the owner, not the car itself.

In Chapter 1, we compared the differences in attributes between matter (physical objects or things) and energy (as feelings or consciousness) to show how their interaction can lead to a *process* of happiness. A similar comparison shows how the interaction of these separate elements is also the origin of our values.

Objects / Things	Feelings / Consciousness
NO INHERENT VALUE	**SOURCE OF ALL VALUE**

We classify values of "good" or "bad" based on their positive or negative effect on our experiences when considered as a whole: the immediate effect, long-range consequences, how many individuals are involved and the differing levels of intensity for each, as a subjective *"evaluation"* of the physical dimension (matter) by the dimension of consciousness (energy) within sentient beings.

The word "good" only means positive experiences, or happiness, whether it comes in the form of a calm spiritual feeling of warmth or peace, or a bubbly enthusiastic thrill, or a sensation of physical pleasure, or any other positive experience. The word "bad" only means negative experience, or misery, in any of its many forms. All valid concepts of "value" must be consistent with the advancement of happiness for sentient beings.[1]

Additional rules, laws, or guidelines can only be relative in value, as suggestions for maximizing happiness in specific situations, according to the differing subjective experiences of each unique individual being or culture-group.

The nature and purpose of conscious experience is to enjoy happiness.

The relationship between how the consciousness subjectively evaluates and interacts with its surrounding environment to engender values is an unbreakable law of the universe, as firm as any law of the physical universe. When people think of the laws of the physical universe, they consider laws that are firm and unchanging, which *cannot be violated*. We can disregard the laws of nature, but we cannot escape the consequences of doing so. But people often think that moral, ethical, or civil laws are different.

We speak of a criminal who "breaks" laws. If he is not caught, we say he got away with it as well. We may dismiss the behavior of small children, or "uncivilized" peoples, and excuse them from accountability, because they "don't know better."

In real life, we cannot "break" the laws of ethics, nor be "excused" from the consequences of trying to do so. What I see in looking around the world is that many people have not learned certain simple facts about living happily that affect their daily lives, and face disastrous emotional consequences. In ethical terms, many people are like a young child who hasn't learned certain laws of nature and freely follows a pretty butterfly over the edge of a deadly cliff. The child meant nothing wrong. The punishment was clearly too severe for the offense. Yet the law of gravity, or any

---

[1]Compare with the Utilitarian concepts of Jeremy Bentham and John Stuart Mill; however, Extro•Dynamics does not attempt any quantification of "pleasure."

other law of nature, is simply a fact of life, and the consequences *will follow* if disregarded, no matter how innocently. Similarly, *the inescapable consequence of following valid ethical principles is happiness!* Failure to observe them leads to the opposite. We must go beyond merely presenting an interesting theoretical discussion of ethical philosophy or simply saying, "thou shalt" this and "thou shalt not" that. We must develop specific, practical guidelines for actually increasing human happiness based on cause-and-effect relationships between actions and consequences.

Making Desires and Values Work Together

The Same Source. In Chapter 1 we saw that satisfying our desire for happiness is based on the interaction between the separate dimensions of matter (objects or things) and energy (as feelings or consciousness). In this chapter we have seen that the source of our values is also based on the same interactive process.

The Same Essence. Our universal desire for happiness can only be satisfied by reaching away from selfish pursuit. Likewise, our universal value of compassion is based on this un-self-ish-ness, which leads to happiness. Our desires and values not only come from the same place, they are of the same essence! They should work together to reinforce each other, not against each other in conflict.

In the science of physics, Albert Einstein recognized the difference between the physical dimension (matter) and the non-physical dimension (energy), and from the interaction of those separate dimensions developed the theory of relativity — unleashing the power of the atom. If we also recognize the differences and inter-relationships between matter and energy (as consciousness), we can also unleash unlimited power!

Chapter 2 Summary:
There is no conflict between moral and ethical standards and enjoying happiness (such as health, wealth or love — or any other form). True ethical values encourage and enhance happiness.

3

Stimulating Selflessness

As we have seen, the dimension of consciousness operates within its surrounding environment, which it depends on for its value and its existence. This environment consists of physical matter as well as other consciousnesses.

Looking back to our earlier example of the interaction between consciousness and matter, we envisioned scattered little "lights" floating through a mostly darkened "physical environment." But from the viewpoint of any individual consciousness, other consciousnesses are also a part of the surrounding environment.

There are *five billion people* on Planet Earth. Within each human mind there exists a uniquely individual dimension of energy, which is the emotional center of awareness. Dr. Leo Buscaglia, a frequent lecturer, says, "I'm awed when I look at an audience or meet people, the gold mine of you. The very fact that I look at you and see all these incredible faces, sparkling eyes and red hair and yellow hair and brown hair and no hair. To say that there are no two of you alike, is awesome." [Buscaglia 1982, p. 191]

To the extent that a person can focus selflessly towards another consciousness, he can reach away from self while, at the same time, tapping directly into that dimension (consciousness) in which all value originates. In the normal process of interpersonal relationships, the inherent value of each consciousness is added together, when each is internalized within the experience of the other.

In the normal course of reaching away from self, as in a hobby or other activity, the consciousness reaches out into the environment for stimulation and activity. The consciousness is operating on the environment unilaterally — a one-way street. A person can enjoy some measure of happiness by becoming "lost" in the outward pull of television, computerized interactions on the Internet or any other activity that draws one's attention away from self-preoccupation. In fact, the way in which these processes cause one to "feel good" or to enjoy the sensations of happiness — sometimes to a point that could almost be described as "addictive" — demonstrates the point very clearly. The biggest problem with such solitary pursuits, however, is that while they draw one away from a conscious preoccupation with self, the solitary nature of these activities simultaneously sets up other subconsciously demanding needs that create additional, subconscious demands for self-directed stimulation and, at the same time, isolate a person from other social interactions.

In the processes of interpersonal relationships, the individual can reach into the environment, and the environment (other consciousnesses) reaches back! The inherent value of each consciousness can nurture and interact with the other, breeding new interactive responses in unlimited possible combinations.

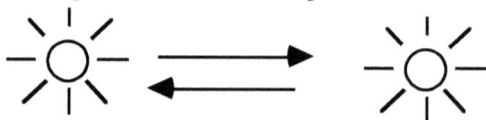

Stimulation from the environment can also include interaction with other consciousnesses

This is why human contact is so fundamental, and why relationships with other human beings are so necessary.

The Extro • Dynamics model originates from these very natural processes of interaction, which are experienced and enjoyed by almost everyone to some degree or other. The people around us are our greatest resource. We can enjoy contacts with other people.

Extro • Dynamics is an enjoyment of the inherent value represented by a consciousness other than our own, for its own intrinsic value, with no self-directed expectation of anything in return. While the process may be initiated and experienced unilaterally, it is actually a form of *sharing* between two separate consciousnesses. It is not a matter of "give and take," as in the reciprocal nature of normal cooperation, but truly of *sharing*. The giving *is* the receiving. We do not subjugate ourselves beneath others; we expand ourselves to embrace others.

In this respect, Extro • Dynamics is different from "cooperation." Cooperation represents separate interests, joining together with an expectation of mutual benefit. This "mutual benefit" can be in the form of accomplishing a shared, common goal, or in achieving the separate, non-conflicting goals of each participant. In either case, combined abilities and efforts enable the achievement of greater results than what each individual could accomplish alone. This is certainly a valid and constructive process of interaction, and basic to many kinds of relationships which people are involved in. Many of our economic and interpersonal relationships are based on legitimate expectations that those relationships are intended to fulfill.

Dawna Markova, writing in the introduction to *Random Acts of Kindness,* tells of her Russian grandmother who explained the different between those who give with the expectation of something in return, and those who give from the heart. Of expectation, she says, "That's not giving, that's trading.... When you give from the heart, it's not to get anything back.... It fills you up. It can't empty you." [Conari Press, 1993, p. 6]

Extro • Dynamics, however, is different from "trading." These lifestyle guidelines are based on the contribution that we extend to others with no expectation of anything in return. It is truly *away from self.* It does not require the participation, cooperation, or even the awareness of the other person.

This is not to say that Extro • Dynamics is some kind of abstraction or far-out hocus-pocus. It is based on natural processes of experience, which allow emotions and feelings and consciousness to flow among separate individuals in ways that everyone normally experiences, but which are developed to a deeper level.

There is a natural flow of consciousness which can bring separate individuals together, and which allows us to have relationships with others. Empathy is a bond of soul alignment that is completely natural to social beings such as humans — the social glue that binds tribes, herds and flocks.

This cognitive affinity for being able to "feel with" others can be manifest in positive, negative or benign forms.

When we encounter another person in an emotion-charged setting, it is natural to get a strong feeling for the other person's experience, and identify it with our own experience through a bond of empathy. Los Angeles Psychiatrist Ronald Podell reports in his book *Contagious Emotions* that mood transmission is real; that moods are "catchy."

This is why a vivid picture of a starving or neglected child can arouse such strong reactions, as people who are otherwise very comfortable feel the child's suffering themselves through the vicarious experience of empathy. The same can also be true of happy feelings. Have you ever heard that "smiling is contagious"...? This process has helped make big money in Hollywood. A skillful writer creates characters which seem so real, through whose eyes a whole set of fictitious experiences are presented, that this natural process allows us to enjoy a "linking up" of the otherwise separate consciousnesses. We used an earlier example of a TV set. What kind of shows do you like to watch on TV? Some fiction? Why do we spend our valuable time watching stories about people we know nothing about, or who never even existed? Or perhaps we enjoy shows such as *Candid Camera, Totally Hidden Video, America's Funniest Home Videos* or the "reality" shows — all of which provide "entertainment" by playing on our natural interest in others' experiences.

Humans are social animals. Like other group animals or birds or fish who congregate in packs, herds, flocks or schools, there is an inherent need for companionship. Dr. Leo Buscaglia has observed, "Love, of some type and degree, is present in all civilized men .... Strong emotions are present in all people. Without feeling, we would not be human." [Buscaglia 1972, p. 95 and p. 102] He further notes, "We are by nature social creatures. Anyone who has ever experienced loneliness — and who hasn't — will agree with that. We need each other." [Buscaglia 1986, p. 54]

As Robinson Crusoe bemoaned in the movie *Man Friday,* "No one can live alone. Solitude tears you to pieces ... You howl to God for the light of a human face."

The nature of empathy, in drawing our interest towards other consciousness, is the mechanism by which this social process operates and by which this need for companionship is satisfied.

Even when this natural processes is corrupted by experiences of frustration, antagonism, or cruelty, it still operates, but in a different form. It may manifest itself in the planning and execution of practical jokes and pranks, which try to *get a reaction* out of someone else. It may show itself in the cruel delight of anticipating the suffering of others, or as nothing more serious than the morbid curiosity of those who slow down to gawk at traffic accidents. What happens if we're watching TV — doing just exactly what we want to be doing — and suddenly, from outside, we hear the *crash, tinkle tinkle* of cars colliding? Do we watch the rest of our show? No! We rush outside to see what happened. Why do we interrupt a planned activity to watch something that has nothing to do with us? Same thing when you're driving on the freeway — there's an accident up ahead, but it's on the other side of the freeway. Why is the traffic on *your* side, which isn't blocked, moving so slowly? It's because people slow down to see what happened. We are naturally curious about others, with an interest in their feelings.

When corrupted in a different way, by wearing down self-esteem or creating feelings of powerlessness, as in the case of the "Stockholm Syndrome," kidnap victims or hostages may form an otherwise inexplicable bond with those responsible for their suffering, or women who suffer from physical or emotional abuse may remain fiercely loyal to their abusers, as reported by psychologist Edna Rawlings [Reported by Shari Roan in *The Los Angeles Times,* 8-20-91, p. E-5].

But when this natural awareness is expressed in positive forms, it enables us to find pleasure in relating to others. As part of a systematic, regular habit, there is no limit to its potential for maximizing happiness in relationships and success in all areas of life.

Other forms of distortion include inappropriate relationship styles, such as co-dependencies, based on mutual weakness rather than strength, which will be discussed later in this book.

Science writer Morton Hunt, in his excellent book *The Compassionate Beast,* discusses the nature and extent to which the development of altruism or compassion is a completely natural aspect of human psychological evolution [Hunt 1990, pp. 41-62].

Nevertheless, some have difficulty accepting the reality that empathy — the foundation on which compassion and altruism are founded — can actually exist.

Some perceive true altruism or true selfless compassion to be impossible, based on two lines of reasoning.

First, some perceive all actions to be, by definition, in one's self interest. However, while this may seem to be reasonable on the surface, no evidence is ever offered to support this assumption other than being able to find a way to explain why their premise is true based on the assumption that their premise is true. This, of course, is nothing more than the logical fallacy of circular reasoning. Just as one can always find some way to "explain" why any action, no matter how unselfish or altruistic it might appear, is really for one's own self-interest, I have heard others, in all seriousness, explain why all actions are really for the purpose of obtaining sex, or are towards the ultimate goal of death, or anything else. Defining the conclusion based on the assumption simply has no logical merit.

The other quasi-rational basis for considering altruistic compassion to be unlikely is because they perceive it to be inconsistent with the evolutionary drive for survival of the individual in order to reproduce and pass their genes forward so those genes are the ones preserved via natural selection based on surviving and reproducing.

But this misunderstands the nature of how genetic traits are passed along to future generations in successful species. No one actually passes their genes to someone else. Your genes never leave your body. What you pass along are partial copies that include information about genetic traits that combine with those from another person, and their traits, to form a new and unique individual.

And the traits you carry, and which (in successful species) are passed on to future generations, are also represented by others in your community or tribe. And the closer they are related to you, the more of those traits you share in common. Thus, while a genetic trait for altruism or compassion may not be necessary for a solitary species, in a social species such a trait for altruism could absolutely confer evolutionary advantage. Example: one individual from a tribe is foraging in the jungle and discovers that a dangerous predator is advancing towards his small village. He can easily escape and save himself — and his genes — or he can terminate the danger but at the expense of his own life. If he sacrifices himself, he will surrender the ability to pass along his own genes, but he will save the lives of many more individuals who carry the same species and familial traits as himself. He will not live to pass along his own genes, but his traits will survive and be passed forward through his community and relatives.

Empathy and compassionate altruism are entirely natural, and observed in all aspects of human nature.

As we saw earlier, this kind of compassionate linking-up, which is the foun-dation on which relationships are built, has long been recognized as a universal value because it is so fundamental to human interactions.

Our discussion so far has been limited to the *underlying concepts*. A formal, conceptual framework is not actually necessary to achieve the Extro • Dynamics lifestyle. In fact, many people have enjoyed the success and happiness of Extro • Dynamics, though they've never even heard of it, by acting on loving, cheerful feelings they found on their own. But the concepts are still helpful, because they introduce us to the idea that there is something better for us, and motivate the desire to learn new habits. But *doing it* must still go beyond the concepts.

Learning Extro • Dynamics is much like learning a foreign language. We can go to classes and work hard to study another language yet, even after many years of difficult, laborious effort, we are awkward and limited in the natural, spontaneous flow of the language. Only when we go beyond formal study, and immerse ourselves in the *process* of using the language, does it become a part of us. In contrast, a little child learns the same language easily, without formal study, by immersion in the spontaneous flow of language around him. Does this mean we shouldn't have formal language study? No, it only means that such study only *introduces* us to the language, and perhaps smoothes out our natural learning process. But such study is only a *help;* it is not a substitute for the real learning that occurs through actual practice.

Chapter 3 Summary

The four simple steps in the Extro • Dynamics model are not only easy to do, but are based on the natural processes of human consciousness which cause us to be social animals with a need for the companionship of others. We must cultivate and expand these natural processes through mutually-nurturing relationships that are: a) based on *active* processes, b) of a *positive* (happy) nature, and c) focused *away from selfish* obsessions.

The Extro • Dynamics™ Lifestyle

We have seen that the process of enjoying happiness in conjunction with achieving our values is based on reaching away from self-preoccupation in a positive way that is consistent with the inherent value of consciousness from which those values originate. We can now build further on the union of these two concepts to develop specific lifestyle guidelines for achieving happiness along with a high standard of values, so that they work together to promote a balanced, harmonious success in all aspects of our personal lives and in the development of public policy.

4

Success Model
for Interactions

The Extro • Dynamics model for successful interactions consists of four simple steps, which can be followed as the example for harmonious interactions in every type of interpersonal encounter. This is *one* model for directing conscious preoccupations away from selfishness, which many have found to be helpful. It is important to note, however, that no claim is made that this is the *only* model for interpersonal happiness. Any form of inter-action that is genu-inely based on an *active* process of *positive, unselfish* interaction with others will lead to the same result. In fact, as noted in the Introduction, there have always been people who have found their own successful techniques for enjoying balanced lifestyles.

Note: While each step is described in detail, keep in mind that, in actual practice, they flow in smooth and rapid succession, as a spontaneous function of our interactions with others.

First Step — Introspection
While the objective of Extro • Dynamics is to reach away from self, the fact still remains that the process of consciousness actually occurs internally. Accordingly, the first perspective from which we have to operate is our own frame of reference.

Does that sound like a contradiction? We just finished a whole discussion about reaching *away* from self. Now I say that the first step is to look inward, towards self value! At this point it's only the starting gate, but for too many people it is also the finish line.

Before we can reach away from self, certain needs must first be met. As in our earlier example of the TV, while the real function is maximized by bringing in stimuli *from beyond self,* the actual operation still occurs *within the set,* which must first be in good working order, or nothing will happen when you turn it on.

We must first understand and appreciate our own value, and take care of certain basic needs. The psychologist Abraham Maslow identified and categorized some of these basic needs when he discussed the various levels which, in his theory of *hierarchies of needs,* we work through to achieve "self-actualization." He demonstrates how the attainment of higher values can only be achieved after a sequence of prerequisite values is first satisfied [Maslow, 1954 pp. 35-104; 1968 pp. 152-154].

Maslow's hierarchy of needs,
from basic survival functions to "Self-Actualization"

The path away from self **starts** from *within the self.* Like the TV, our own "receivers" have to be in good working order. As part of the first step, there are certain general things that we can do on an ongoing basis. Some of those basic needs include physical health and well-being, and avoiding situations which could cause disease, injury or pain which force our attention toward self-preoccupation. Also, we must take care of our mental and emotional health. We have to identify and avoid those conditions that cause stress, pressure, worry and depression, which force our attention towards ourselves in unpleasant ways. We have to develop knowledge and skills, so that as we go on to the other steps we have the skills necessary to do so effectively.

Dr. Leo Buscaglia, perhaps the leading proponent of unselfish love in modern times, also notes with emphasis that we cannot love others until we first build a foundation of primary self love [Buscaglia 1982, p. 9-10; 1972 p. 18 and pp. 135-144].

Even Jesus, the ultimate teacher of compassionate love, who in Matthew 22:36-40 and Luke 10:25-37 cited the Old Testament command to "love your neighbor as yourself"[1] as one of the two "Great Commandments," emphasized the need to love your neighbor *as yourself* (and then used the parable of the Good Samaritan to define "neighbor" quite broadly). He did not say to put yourself down, or love your neighbor more than yourself, but clearly recognizes that true love of others emanates from, and is inextricably bound with, love of self. Compassionate love does not mean merely *giving,* it means *sharing.* It is not the subjugation of self beneath others; it is the expansion of self to embrace others. To "Love your neighbor *as* yourself," does not mean "love your neighbor instead of (or above) yourself." Love of self is not selfish, it is the springboard to expanding beyond the single limited dimension of our own selves to an infinite sharing of self value with the unlimited value of the infinite range of consciousness of which we are a part, and which we expand and elevate ourselves to a capacity such that we can receive it.

In order to reach selflessly towards the value of other *consciousness* in the surrounding environment, we must understand and appreciate what that value is. Again, by starting from this perspective we know best — our own frame of reference — we can recognize and appreciate the special and unique value that we represent. We cannot experience or understand the feelings of love — of *compassionate joy* — from the bottom of an empty cup.

---

[1]Leviticus 19:18

When our "cup runneth over," then it will spill into the lives of others and we can truly and unselfishly reach away from self.

We must believe in ourselves. We must be able to visualize ourselves as compassionate individuals able to enjoy positive interactions with the people around us.

We must appreciate our own self-worth, and feel self-confidence and self-esteem before we can enjoy the same kind of special value and unique self-worth in others. As a first step only, it is not the same as self-preoccupation or self-obsession, which are ends unto themselves. This first step allows for the necessary care of one's being and development of necessary skills and talents to operate effectively. In Extro • Dynamics, this provides for a recognition of the value of consciousness and of the Self, and an awareness that even those feelings, which may originate from beyond the self, but will actually be experienced internally.

The first step is: stop and consider for a moment just the importance of your own personal value. Also consider the reality and intensity of your own dimension of consciousness. Specifically identify occasions on which you had particularly strong experiences with different types of feelings.

The first few times through this exercise, you may want to actually make a list of each type of event, to actually *go through* a complete visualization of your experience in each one:

Embarrassment — think back to a specific event where you were caught doing something that you weren't supposed to, or accidentally did something that you didn't mean to, or had something happen to you in front of others that left you feeling embarrassed, which can be a particularly intense and biting emotion.

I'll share with you an experience I had with embarrassment back in the 7th grade. I was 13 years old. At that age you're just beginning to develop an adult personality, and you're becoming very conscious of how other people perceive you, and your social interactions — especially in front of peers — are very crucial. If you get embarrassed in front of your peers at 13 you are *very* embarrassed.

In the 7th grade, I decided to run for student council. One of the requirements was to give a campaign speech, which had to be memorized. So I wrote out a short speech and memorized it. I practiced it and practiced it until my whole family was sick of hearing it — until it was thoroughly committed to my memory, and probably theirs.

On the day of the speech, the entire 7th grade was herded into the junior high auditorium, and the candidates were seated in a row of seats on the stage as we awaited our turns to speak.

My speech went something like this... "You don't have to vote for me, Douglas Dunn..." — see, I wanted to get in some early name recognition — "...but let me give you a few reasons why you should," and then I was to go on and recite all the reasons why they should vote for me.

When it was my turn to speak, I trotted over to the podium, and I started my little speech. "You don't have to vote for me, Douglas Dunn," I began. "But let me give you a few reasons why you should." Then, all of a sudden, my mind went blank. Frozen in the mental paralysis of self-preoccupation, I couldn't remember any of the reasons why they should vote for me. I just stood there. I couldn't think of anything to say, and I finally had to slink sheepishly back to my seat where I could still see the whole crowd, all looking at me. Embarrassment. A most stinging sensation.

By the way, I didn't win the election.

But as I recall that experience, it reminds me of how alive and intense and real and special my process of consciousness is. It *was* a very strong feeling.

Of course, strong feelings don't have to be negative! I often suggest starting with negative feelings, to get them out of the way first and because their stinging sharpness makes them easy to recall with vivid intensity. But it is important to move on to other feelings that are pleasant, and focus the power of our intentions in positive directions, and which are equally strong:

Awe and wonder at the beauties of Nature, great or small. Think back to when you saw and appreciated the majestic panoramas of the Grand Canyon. Or great geysers. Or vast open mountains or forests. Have you ever enjoyed the tropical beauty of Hawaiian beaches, surrounded by nearby mountains with caves and waterfalls and lush foliage that make you feel as if you're in the Garden of Eden? What about something small, like a bird's nest, or a butterfly alighting on a flower, or a spider gently and meticulously spinning its web?

Romance: Joy in romance; disappointment in romance. Think of the excitement and anticipation of new love, and the thrill of romantic sharing as it unfolds when it is good. But think also of those times when it's not good, when relationships break up amidst feelings of disappointment or betrayal, with anguish and suffering so intense that you thought no other human being could ever have suffered so much.

What about **career**? Think about the joy of a unique contribution that made you stand out and earned you special recognition — some achievement or discovery on the job, or some other satisfying success, that made you special. In contrast, think of the gut-wrenching and terrifying insecurity of being without a job, or the sense of failure and humiliation when you lost a job.

We have all had traumas and crises that seemed too much to bear, and which reaffirmed our great capacity for depth of feeling. Whether it be personal tragedies in relationships, confrontations with illnesses or disease, or economic insecurity, these experiences test our emotional endurance. When we just look through our own perspective, we feel that no one else could ever have suffered so intensely. We say, *"Why me?"* But we have also had successes, achievements and good times. Keep a remembrance of such experiences — both good and bad— ready at your "mental fingertips" so you can quickly recall and reaffirm the unique and special value of your existence. The first step really means that you have to love yourself.

It is okay to start with negative examples, to remember them as an affirmation of the reality and intensity of our feelings. As part of a *positive, active* process, we can also go back and re-enact these negative experiences in our minds, inserting different endings in which we achieve happier outcomes, by considering how we could have responded differently and then visualizing ourselves as handling it a better way, to remind ourselves that we now have the ability to make things turn out right.

But I recommend finishing up with *positive* examples, to reaffirm *value* in ourselves and leave us feeling good, with the power of mental imaging focused in positive energy. We all have good as well as bad experiences. If we leave our minds focused on the good, that is what we will be attracted to, and we will dwell on that which is positive and cheerful, in the *positive* nature that is fundamental to Extro • Dynamics.

In most cases, individuals can use these positive affirmations and visualizations to look at their own lives, put their feelings in perspective and, with conscious effort, enjoy the value of their own selves. Yet there are some people whose early experiences have been filled with violence, abuse, hopelessness and messages of inferiority to the extent that their ability to feel good about themselves is severely handicapped. Before they can love themselves, as the first step toward reaching out and loving others, it is necessary to reverse or undo those early negative influences. If such people are not capable of doing this on their own, then they may require assistance from self-help groups or professional counseling in achieving the first step.

Even so, to a less serious extent, all of us may get upset with ourselves from time to time over some silly blunder we may make, but that's because we aren't perfect. Love does not require perfection. It only requires awareness, appreciation and a celebration of inherent and uniquely special value.

Important note: while it is recommended that the steps be followed in order, it does not require perfect mastery before moving on to the next step. *Go through each step as well as you can, and move on to the next step.* In time, as you go through the steps, your skill will improve. There will always be room for improvement. But, if you intend to wait until you master the first step before moving on to the next, you will never achieve it; you will spend your whole life, as so many others do, dwelling only on self-directed obsessions.

Second Step — Neutraspection

After you have developed the real understanding that *you* are someone special and important, from the perspective of your own frame of reference, you can start moving away from the starting point of Self, to *Beyond Self.*

This requires seeing the world from a different frame of reference, which is often difficult at first. Even when the obstacles to self-love have been overcome, through our own efforts or with professional help, we still operate through the perspectives of our own consciousness. No matter how selflessly-directed we become, our own consciousness is still the channel through which our perceptions are filtered. We need to develop a more objective framework through which to process these perceptions.

Look around and visualize your present immediate environment as you would normally see it.

Now, for the perspective of the second step, imagine that you are viewing it, not from your actual present viewpoint, but from a neutral viewpoint, outside yourself, in which you can see not only the people and objects around you, but you can also see *yourself* from a detached, outside perspective as *part of* the environment rather than as the *observer* of the environment.

We have now begun to move from the starting point of Self (after the basic, prerequisite needs have been met) to *beyond self,* to a higher place *that is directed away from self* — to see yourself in a neutral, detached way that is not personal to yourself nor to any other specific person. Others are not *more* special nor are they *less* special. They are *equally* special and important in their own unique ways.

If we continue to borrow from the idea of Maslow's hierarchy, then the upper levels of the hierarchy could be adapted as follows to include the additional dimension:

In some ways, the second step is the easiest. It is simple and straightforward — just move outside the limiting paradigms of self-preoccupation into a perception where we are *part of,* not the *center of,* the surrounding environment.

When self needs have been reasonably satisfied, one can find fulfillment <u>beyond self</u>, through Extro • Dynamics

In other ways it is the most difficult, because the mental habits that confine us to that self-directed perspective may be stronger and harder to break than we imagine. We may need tools of meditation, interactive group support and other mental exercises to help us break out of this mold, but it is the key to success in the steps that follow. Developing a sense of humor also helps to break out of the trap of self-preoccupation, into a neutral but pleasant external state. The key is to use whatever mental and psychic tools possible (those we already have as well as new ones we can develop) to break into that external, neutral step.

Third Step — Extrospection

In the third step of Extro • Dynamics, the perspectives of the first two steps can be integrated, leading to a more subjective, personal viewpoint without being centered around self-preoccupation.

Having achieved the detached, objective frame of reference from the second step, we can now develop a more specific focus, in a way that enables the linking up with other consciousness.

Glance around toward some other person. Anyone. Watch the person very closely. Realize that within this being there is a special world of feelings and experiences which is just as real, and just as intense, as your own. Glance over at your perception of yourself as seen from your external viewpoint, and see how you are so much the same as your human brother or sister, both so special and unique, and glance back at the other person.

Remember the little exercise that we went through when we celebrated our own unique value. We considered the types of experiences that we've gone through, both positive and negative: embarrassment, joy in romance, failure in romance, success on the job, celebrations of the beauty of nature and a unique pattern of experiences that weave together to make our own special lifetime pattern.

Now look at this other person. That person also represents a unique pattern of experiences woven together in a special way that is unique and exciting. Just like yours, these experiences are both negative and positive.

Think of the fears, the joys, the pains, and the desires of this human brother or sister. When we look at our own personal tragedies and say, *"Why me?"* it is because we are so self-preoccupied that we think we are the only one who could ever have suffered so much. But in fact, we have all had those *"Why me?"* experiences more than once. Every one of us! Every human being has their own problems, traumas, or crises to deal with — either as acute, immediate difficulties or as ongoing problems. Each person also has joys and pleasures that are uniquely their own. What are the joys and sorrows of this unique and special brother or sister? What are the *Why me?'s* in this person's life … and, what are the special celebrations of joy and success he has enjoyed?

Visualize the same kinds of intense feelings in the life and experiences of this other person as you did in great detail when you recalled the intensity of your own feelings in the first step. Don't forget that these feelings and experiences are no less real just because they occur within a different consciousness. Here is a whole dimension that has developed its own fascinating pattern of experiences, and you might only have been marginally aware that it even existed! Just like yours, this world is very important. Just like yours, these feelings are special and unique, and important *for their own sakes*. Just because you can't actually crawl into this other mind and feel those experiences doesn't make them any less real. Pain is pain and joy is joy, and it is the same whether experienced within your consciousness or someone else's.

As with your own life, remember that the life of this other person includes both good and bad. Let your understanding and acceptance include the whole range of experience. But, as with yourself, finish with an awareness of something positive. *Everyone* has both the good and the bad. If we look for the good we will find it, and by dwelling on the *positive* we affirm a warm and cheerful closeness that allows us to reach away from self more easily.

Open yourself to feeling receptive to the Spirit of other consciousnesses. Recognize the "little lights" of consciousness as being distinct and separate from the "darkness" of the surrounding physical environment, and let yourself be receptive to the value inherent in each such light.

Look into the eyes of the other person. Imagine yourself as occupying the physical place where he is. But instead of looking at the world through *your* point of view, as we did in the first step, or the detached, objective viewpoint of the second step, look through the vantage point of *the other person.*

Visualize various objects as they would appear from this other person's vantage point. Try to imagine subtle differences in the way things might appear from *that* perspective instead of from where you actually are. Try to imagine how *you* look to *them!* Try to really put yourself in the physical place where they are. Not just in the way things might *look* differently — how do they sound? What is that person hearing? What does that person smell? What about sensations of touch? Feel the air or sun or wind on their skin. What are they touching? Holding? Take the time to thoroughly explore the immediate physical environment as it would appear through the perspective of another person's senses.

Then, carefully evolve your way into an exploration of their immediate mental and *emotional* environment. Imagine all the little thoughts and feelings that might make up their present experience. Try to visualize the operation of the outer environment on their present moment of consciousness, as all the little sensations are woven together into a developing process of experience. Without knowing specific details, let yourself feel curious as to what the traumas and crises, joys and pleasures are in the life of that other person, *the way that person feels them.*

Let yourself recognize conditions of *mood,* which color the brightness and flavor of that little "light" of consciousness. Is it happy? Content? Angry? Frustrated? Be aware of those *transitory* aspects of consciousness that we can often discern clearly by watching for them receptively.

Some believe that personality is influenced by genetically-inherited traits, while others believe it is learned through environmental influences and most believe it involves some combination of both. If studying the psychology of how these forces interact enhances your empathetic bonding with others, then exploring such methods might be very helpful.

Some believe that the natal position of the sun, moon and planets, as charted in astrological horoscopes, provides information about personality traits; others believe that our present condition is shaped by the karma of past lives, and others believe in still other religious, cosmic and metaphysical forces. It is not the purpose of this book to promote or challenge such beliefs. Whatever tools will help you focus on who and what another person is all about can find a role in helping those who find constructive ways to employ them.

The combination of physical, mental and emotional perspectives can be synthesized into a completeness of the person's *spiritual* perspective. Get inside this other mind until you identify those feelings with your own so they become an extension of yourself.

But also be aware of the great extent of unique lifetime experiences and of deeper levels of feeling and real personality beyond your superficial observation, and be aware of how much brightness and value you are exposed to which is beyond what you can perceive. Feel their feelings! Let the value of your unique consciousness merge with the equal value that can be drawn selflessly through the feelings, values and perspectives of another unique consciousness. Reach out and really share the spiritual value of another being.

Some have expressed concern that some people might resent this as an "intrusion" into the privacy of consciousness. The feelings of Extro • Dynamics do not require anything that would make someone else feel uncomfortable. It is your own experience — a tool for utilizing human resources to draw yourself away from selfishness. It imposes nothing on the other person. Extro • Dynamics will open up new potentials for spiritual value, but it won't make you a mind-reader.

Dr. Leo Buscaglia notes, "The word, empathy, ... is still a great word. It means to 'feel' with. It does not imply 'total understanding.' We know that we can never really understand another person." He goes on to discuss the positive ways in which empathetic love still holds the key to bringing separate lives together. Separately, he notes, "This does not mean that we can completely empathize with another's feelings and behaviors. It is painful to me when I hear someone say, 'I know just how you feel!' One does not! One never can! At best, we are able to understand only what we have truly experienced, and each experience is always very personal. But when we understand our own personal conflicts and feelings based upon general human experience we can begin to understand how others may feel. It is this point at which compassion begins." [Buscaglia 1978, p. 130; and 1972 p. 166]

To the extent that you are acquainted with background information about the person you have some advantage in understanding, sharing and *feeling* their perspective, but you can still reach away from self to the *perspectives* of other thoughts and feelings in a manner that is speculative and appreciative of potentials, without intruding into specific details.

It is not necessary that this empathetic perspective provide knowledge of what another person actually feels, or even (as Dr. Buscaglia suggests) what they *might* feel. The point is that it draws us close to them, yet asks nothing of them. It enables a merging of their interests with ours, their value with ours, even though the entire process occurs within our own experience, but imposes nothing on them. It draws us together, and opens up new horizons of spiritual treasure. Ironically, it is the gateway of unselfishness, yet is also the doorway to our own personal enrichment.

The key is to develop and utilize all abilities, resources and energies possible to expand the natural human capacity for empathetic linking with others of our species in ways that bring us together at a level of depth beyond the usual level of our experience. But having achieved this state of *feeling* or *perception,* we must take one more step to transform it into something real in a world that also consists of physical and tangible realities.

Fourth Step — Action

The first three steps, taken together, set up a selfless focus of attention based on cognitive and sensory *perspectives*. Feelings. The fourth step is to *do something* — a behavioral response. You could never be found guilty of a crime or an evil deed merely for *thinking* about it; so also kind thoughts or warm feelings alone will not make you a compassionate person. Active realism transforms idealism into a balanced lifestyle.

Rodgers and Hammerstein wrote, "A bell is no bell 'til you ring it. A song is no song 'til you sing it. Love in your heart wasn't put there to stay. Love isn't love 'til you give it away." Love does not exist until one person not only feels positive, unselfish feelings for another, but goes on to express them in a specific action.

In *The Road Less Traveled,* Dr. M. Scott Peck goes so far as to say that love doesn't even exist as long as it remains just a feeling. There is no love until there is sufficient *will* to express those feelings in *action*. [Peck, pp. 116-120].

After completing the first three steps in detail, your feelings will be in a very different place towards the other person. At this point, it is natural that new behavior patterns will emerge. When loving, empathetic feelings are truly enjoyed, it will be natural to respond with loving, empathetic behavior. You will not only share *feelings,* but you will also feel motivated to *do* something to contribute to that process of joyful caring. Specific behavior details will vary from situation to situation, and will be handled differently to reflect the personalities of those you interact with. But as you begin to appreciate and share the unique value in each person around you, you will also seek to develop the behavioral response that is uniquely right for that individual and situation.

Sometimes the response will be warm, affectionate, and demonstrative. The action may be in a tangible form — actually *doing* something to cheer someone up or brighten the moment of interaction that you share, or helping someone solve a problem. It may be in the form of conversation — saying the right thing to add cheerfulness or sunshine, or careful listening to what someone else needs to share. In conversational responses, be direct and specific. If you offer a compliment, make it sincere and specific; if you are listening, watch the person and ask questions. If your first three steps are genuine, and you are truly linked to the other person's perspective, you will do this naturally. Sometimes, the response will be more passive, to avoid making the other person feel uncomfortable. Sometimes, the response will be of quiet appreciation only, and will not be reflected in overt behavior.

Some might ask, why waste the effort of going through the first three steps? Why not just *do something* for those we encounter?

Without these preliminary steps we might not be motivated to *do* anything. These steps make the fourth step—*action*—a natural, automatic consequence, and also affect the *nature* of our response. They ensure that our actions are truly selfless, not just something that's really for our own benefit. How many times do people "do something for others" out of duty or obligation rather than from real, spontaneous and joyful caring? How many times are people annoyed by intrusive "do-gooders" who do what they think others should need rather than what others really want or need?

I remember an event that occurred when I was just beginning to practice this model myself. I saw a little old lady walking down the street, struggling to carry several large grocery bags. In my enthusiasm to "do something," I rushed over and offered to carry the bags. I hadn't fully viewed the situation *from her perspective*. How would it look to someone old and defenseless to be suddenly rushed by a young man in his early twenties asking to take her bags? Fearfully, and without resistance, she let me take the groceries. I quickly realized my mistake, but the damage was already done. I had offered to help and could not gracefully take my offer back. Quietly I took the bags and carried them to her house. She was tense and quiet all the way. When we got to her house, I returned her groceries to her. By now she must have been reassured that I was not going to attack or rob her, but she offered me money as if to anticipate other possible motives. I refused, and left her with my best wishes. But I also learned a lesson. Looking *through the other person's perspective*, we must understand their fears, their dignity and pride. We must make sure we respond to what *they* really need or feel.

While it is usually more effective to follow the steps in order, there are occasions when we have difficulty going through the *feelings* of the first three steps. In such cases, as well as special conditions of pathology, *if we remain focused on the goal of combining both feelings and actions,* it is sometimes helpful to just start with compassionate actions, and go through the motions — "fake it" 'til you can "make it" — continuing to work on both, until the feelings and actions both kick into gear and reinforce each other. If you just can't get the feelings to kick in first, at least going through the motions, superficially at first, and manifesting compassionate kindness to others, can have a transformative effect on not just our feelings, but our basic character, such that the actions can habituate us to feeling emotional capacities we never before realized were possible.

Just as our empathetic interest in other consciousness can be either positive or negative, so can our actions. A person may take actions that *seem* to benefit another person, but really try to hurt or dominate them or take advantage of them. (If we are acting out of ulterior motives of self interest, we are not really reaching away from self. We are still driven by *expectations.* We need to let ourselves get caught up in a selfless perspective, by going through each step carefully.) A person might interact with others from a position of weakness (as in "co-dependency") or let others take advantage of them or treat them like a doormat. As we will discuss in Chapters 5 and 6 on implementing the model, the compassion of Extro • Dynamics never requires us to accept behavior in others that hurts themselves or others, or which compromises individual autonomy. On the contrary, by approaching behavioral responses *after* going through the first three steps, we can find behavioral responses that truly reach away from self-preoccupation or expectations in a *positive* approach to *constructive sharing.*

Even *perfect* feelings would not always lead to perfect behavior, simply because we don't always know what is the right action or we don't do it right. Developing positive behavioral responses is a separate skill, which will increase through regular practice.

In the transition from perspectives and feelings to behavior, just relax and be yourself: be positive and cheerful and let yourself *smile*. Picture yourself as responding the way a successful role model might act. Visualize ways in which your interaction could add to the cheerfulness or playfulness of that other person, and let your actions flow in harmony with what you visualized. You will treat people in a way that reflects the positive sharing of feelings that has occurred.

The essence of Extro • Dynamics is *action!* As with all things, we learn it best by *doing it.* Learn love by doing loving things.

In the words of Dr. Leo Buscaglia: " 'To be is to do,' says the existentialist. 'One only becomes real (human) at the point of action.' " [Buscaglia 1972, p. 115]. Throughout his lectures, books and tapes, Dr. Leo offers many excellent and innovative suggestions for specific ways in which to bridge the link between inspirational motivation and the behavioral aspects of expressing compassionate love. One of his most innovative strategies for creative, loving *action* invites participation from others. His "Felice Foundation[1]," provides assistance for unselfish, loving projects.

Once the behavioral patterns are developed, it is just a matter of expanding them into all areas of involvement with others. Interactions with other human beings are a part of almost every setting in which we function. Other people are a part of *everything we do.* True Extro • Dynamics is not just sharing this *active extrospection* once in a while, but in using these techniques to draw out the unique personal value in *every encounter.*

Extro • Dynamics is just a cheerful habit of enjoying the people around us — unconditionally and without expectation. Mastery of Extro • Dynamics means you can glide through life's daily pattern of interactions, freed from self-preoccupation, continually recharged by all the surrounding spiritual wealth.

---

[1]Named from the Italian word meaning "happiness," which was also his given name at birth; his very name celebrates the joy of compassion! For information about Felice Foundation, write to P.O. Box 599, Glenbrook, NV 89413.

Summary of the Model

The Extro • Dynamics model is easy to remember, and easy to do. Keep it in mind, and in *action,* as you approach each interaction with another person, and you will be amazed at the way it changes your perceptions, your feelings, your actions towards others and your outlook for success.

Chapter 4 Summary

The Extro • Dynamics model is very simple. All you have to do is:

1. **Introspection:** Have good feelings about yourself, and keep yourself in good shape [take care of basic needs, and celebrate your own unique value].

2. **Neutraspection:** Move away from the usual perspective of a self-centered viewpoint, into a neutral, detached frame of reference and visualize the surrounding environment as a *part of* it, rather than as the *observer* of it.

3. **Extrospection:** Reach out in a cheerful way to the value and feelings of someone else through a perception of the world from *their* perspective, in a combination that is greater than what either perspective could represent separately [explore and share the same value in another person].

4. **Action:** Make a specific, positive, cheerful behavioral contribution to the interaction.

The steps begin with **self-value,** lead **away from self-preoccupation** and into an **active process of energy.**

Again, though we have presented the steps separately, and in great detail, in actual practice they run seamlessly together in spontaneous, rapid succession.

5

Making it Work

As you cultivate your own regular and habitual practice of the Extro • Dynamics model, you'll find that the steps themselves are not
hard to do. But you will also find that remembering to have these
steps operating actively in every encounter with others takes per-
sistence and practice until it becomes a habitual, automatic
response. Let's look at ways in which we can make this model a
practical and successful guide to interpersonal encounters.

Let's first explore a specific example of the steps in detail, and
then examine the kinds of resistance we might feel and how to
overcome them.

A Specific Example

Here's an example I developed while driving along the freeway,
going northbound on the Hollywood Freeway, from downtown Los
Angeles to the San Fernando Valley. I'm just north of Highland
Avenue. It's a hot summer day, about 5:30 in the afternoon. The
traffic is fairly heavy, and moving slowly. It's rush hour and people have just gotten off work. I'm driving a small sub-compact car
in the far right lane. Right behind me is a big truck, with a big
burly truck driver behind the wheel. In front of me is a yellow
Mustang convertible with two young ladies sitting in front, chat-
ting casually, enjoying the sunshine, apparently not too concerned
with the traffic. To my left is a silver BMW, with a well-groomed
man about 40 alone in the car, looking very businesslike. He seems

to be in kind of a hurry, perhaps on his way home from work and impatient with the traffic.

In applying Extro • Dynamics in this situation, the first step involves only myself. Much of this first step, taking care of myself physically, mentally and emotionally, is an ongoing process that should always be operating in the background of my life. It doesn't require specific action in this situation. But I will want to reaffirm the more specific aspects of the first step, the celebration of myself, the appreciation of myself, the enjoyment of myself, again reviewing the intensity and reality of my own positive and negative feelings, and the way they weave together into my own unique pattern of experiences which make me different from any other human being. I always keep these ready at my "mental fingertips." I visualize myself as a compassionate person who finds constructive ways to enjoy positive interactions with the people around me.

Next, I will break free from the constraints of my own self-centered perspective. I might use one (or more) of many mental techniques to achieve this. Perhaps I will imagine the disembodied essence of myself drifting above my car and looking down on the situation from a detached, neutral perspective, where I am a part of the scene, not the observer of it. I will see myself sitting in my car, and the other drivers in their vehicles, all as equal parts of the situation. While this might seem deceptively simple, it is the key toward breaking free of self-preoccupation that is a crucial component of linking up with other consciousness.

After I have successfully gotten "outside myself," I will reach out and extend that same value I recognize in myself to someone else. In this situation, I am surrounded by a wealth of opportunities. In fact, fully taking advantage of this opportunity can turn the unpleasantness of traffic into a cheerful celebration of life. I could extend this value towards any one of the people that surrounds me or, one by one, I could extend it to all of them.

I move out of the perspective of my own viewpoint, and try to visualize the scene from a detached, neutral frame of reference, as an observer instead of a participant. I try to visualize how things look from above the scene on the freeway. I look at myself as just another one of the drivers stuck in the traffic.

I select one of them — maybe the truck driver behind me. In the same detail as I did for myself, I recognize and appreciate that his special pattern of experiences is also of unique and equal value.

I will now combine the unique value that I represent with the value of this other person. I can imagine myself as experiencing this encounter through the physical perspective he occupies. How do things look, visually, from his point of view instead of mine? I look back at the truck driver. He's sitting in a much higher spot than I am. He looks at traffic from a different viewpoint than I do; the cars look different from his higher vantage point. I can look down on myself and imagine and visualize how I might look from his point of view.

What other sights and sounds and smells do I see and hear and smell right now, and how is the frame of reference of this other driver similar or different than mine?

Then I can develop that perspective into an exploration of his mental and emotional environments. I can try to imagine the thoughts and feelings that make up his present experience. As we've already mentioned, Extro • Dynamics will not make me a mind reader. But I can first observe and I can be aware of those transitory aspects of consciousness that we call mood. Is he happy, content, angry, frustrated? Those things I probably can determine. From there I can explore further. What kind of person is he? He looks big and burly. Is he a tough guy or just a big ol' Teddy bear? At this point I must be careful to avoid stereotypes based on appearance and other superficial factors. Until my interaction leads me to know more about what he is really like, I must acknowledge that I don't know. But I can explore the depth and potential and look for more substantial clues. If he gives me an obscene gesture I may conclude that he is disagreeable and tough. If so, why? What influences might have caused him to learn feelings and behavior that are counterproductive? Or maybe that is superficial, too. He may be a wonderful person whose *mood* — the transitory aspect of feeling — is momentarily unpleasant.

The only thing I really do know about him is that he is a truck driver in traffic behind a tiny sub-compact. But that is not insignificant information. What is it like to drive a truck for a living on the Southern California freeways? What kind of pressure is he under to meet deadlines and schedules? How does he feel about little cars that block his way? What I *can* absolutely understand is the complexity of this interaction — how much potential is here; how much value I've encountered from this single light of consciousness, which even surpasses what I can perceive.

As I develop this perspective to deeper and deeper levels, I can be drawn away from myself, out of the limitations of my own perspective. I can let myself feel a warmth and closeness toward this stranger, as if he is a dear friend — as if he is an extension of my own value. As long as I'm directed away from myself, enjoying the value and closeness of this new anonymous friend, I can no longer be annoyed by the traffic; I'm not drawn into the self-preoccupation of my own frustrations. Even the other people can't bother me.

Maybe the truck driver is following too close. Maybe as traffic picks up and the cars are going faster, that might become a safety hazard. But now my response can be more constructive. Instead of getting pissed off, I can respond cheerfully, to solve the problem instead of to vent useless frustrations. Because I no longer perceive this person as a stranger, I can treat the person the way I would anybody else that would be close to me; if my friend or my sister or one of my co-workers was following too close, I would communicate constructively a message to solve the safety problem, but I wouldn't get angry or lose my temper at them.

Having completed the third step towards this truck driver, I can either move on to the fourth step, action, or repeat the process towards those in the other cars nearby.

As I develop an intense level of warm feelings for those around me, it is natural for me to follow through with an appropriate behavioral response. The appropriate response varies in each situation, and toward each person. The way I relate to the impatient businessman in the BMW may be very different than to the casual, relaxed young ladies in the convertible. Sometimes it will be very direct, and other times restrained, to avoid making people feel uncomfortable. Often the response will just be a quiet appreciation of others with no opportunity to actually do something.

In this case, it may be tempting to dismiss it as a situation that doesn't require an active response. Here we are, stuck in traffic. The people surrounding me are all strangers. I've never seen them before, and I'll probably never see them again. We're in separate cars. It doesn't seem that we really have any direct interaction. But that's not really true. And if I'm really at a place of feeling close to each of those nearby, I can find many creative opportunities to make a cheerful contribution. I can watch for ways to ease the flow of traffic. I can make room for others. As needed, I can communicate with other drivers in cheerful gestures that build them up and solve problems, instead of making already tense feelings even worse. I can be careful to avoid actions that may be interpreted as being rude or careless. There are lots of things we can do to constructively smooth out the frustrations and irritations of traffic.

As we can see, the steps themselves are easy to do, when we actually make a conscious effort to go through each step.

A Lifestyle Habit
After you get used to the steps, they are not really complicated or cumbersome or lengthy. You can glide quickly and spontaneously from one to the next. But in the beginning, trying to apply this model in every situation of interpersonal involvement, you won't feel as if you're "gliding through life's daily pattern of interactions..." The smooth, habitual enjoyment of Extro • Dynamics will only come with time and practice. At first, conscious effort may be required through each step. But ultimately, we can move away from conscious, intellectual control over the process. A smooth, spontaneous habit is not consciously controlled by mental or intellectual effort, but a natural approach to interactions. It is a simple sequence of perceptions and actions, quickly executed, that make a lifetime of difference in all our interactions with others. The mind and intellect can initiate the conditions, and set the process in motion, but it must then flow in feeling and spirit.

The steps themselves are easy to do when you make a conscious effort to get started. The difficulty is in overcoming the resistance to doing it when you just don't feel like it, and setting up an adequate schedule of *practice*, until the feelings become part of an automatic, spontaneous practice of *spirit*. Although this early conscious, mental control may initially reduce the spontaneous enjoyment you will achieve later, it does provide a starting point.

Take the time to get a clear overview of your present activities. Write out a schedule of your present lifestyle, if necessary, to see how you budget your time. It should not be necessary to make any great changes in your lifestyle — Extro • Dynamics can fit into any cultural setting or system of personal preferences — but you will have to get a feeling for what your schedule involves in order to fit Extro • Dynamics in.

In your schedule, identify those time slots which already are committed to fixed obligations, such as work, school, or other regular activities, so you can determine how and when you can add Extro • Dynamics as a part of those fixed activities. Perhaps on your coffee break at work, you can observe the people around you. Perhaps in dealing with clients or customers, you can add Extro • Dynamics to enrich those encounters beyond what is otherwise expected. In the school environment, Extro • Dynamics can be used to enhance the interactions with teachers and students.

Identify other aspects of your life that are more flexible, and in those also set aside specific periods of time when you can use the model. It is also important to identify conditions or situations that make it most difficult, so you can give special attention in those situations.

At various times, and in various settings, on your practice schedule and otherwise, look around you. Identify several specific individuals. In the office lunchroom they may be well-known co-workers; at the park or beach, they may be strangers; in the market, they may be other shoppers that you pass by. These people can be people you know or people you don't know; they can be men or women; they can be grownups or children; they can be anyone — of any size, shape, color, or background. All are important, and all have consciousness and feelings you can enjoy. Unknown to each of them, go through all four of the steps.

Over a period of time, these practice experiences can be developed into a natural part of all your moment-by-moment feelings, directing your perceptions away from yourself, and encouraging behavior to cause greater happiness for yourself and those whose feelings are important to you. Most important is that you not just think about Extro • Dynamics as a theoretical concept, but that you actually go out and *start doing it!*

In order to develop the habit of *doing it,* get into a habit of daily reminders to practice. Perhaps in conjunction with the first step — ongoing reaffirmation of self-value — start each day with a reaffirmation of your commitment to yourself and others, and a reminder that, just for today, you will look for *and find* the opportunities to put this model into practice.

Working With Others

Often it is not enough for us to try and remember the Extro • Dynamics lifestyle on our own. We need stronger ongoing support, which can be found in working with others, whether they are new beginners or more advanced. This mutual support can take place in the course of other personal-development activities or self-help organizations, or by meeting for this specific purpose. Individuals helping each other by practicing together, or providing regular feedback and support, helps develop and solidify this daily lifestyle habit in three important ways:

First, working with others who are more experienced provides role models of the success that comes from practicing these life-style habits. For example, you may have encountered a particular situation that seems impossible. Others who are detached from the situation can look at it from a neutral point of view and offer suggestions that you may have missed. Working with others helps you to monitor your growth in relation to others, and lets you share in the experiences of how others have been able to overcome the obstacles that sometimes arise. We need the reinforcement of sharing success experiences with others, and their suggestions for overcoming obstacles.

Second, in the emotional heat of real-life experiences, we are sometimes too close to the situation to think objectively, or things just happen too fast to develop a rational plan for how to respond with Extro • Dynamics. We cannot always see the ways in which we are missing opportunities to enjoy the value of others. Often, just by describing problematic situations to someone else in a safe environment, we can focus on them more thoughtfully than in the heat of the actual experience, and obvious solutions become apparent even before someone else makes a suggestion. Yet if we had not articulated them openly to another person, we would not have seen them on our own.

Third, the process of interaction with others is at the very core of the Extro • Dynamics lifestyle (See Chapters 1-3). For beginners, the interaction with others helps draw them into a selfless orientation, away from self preoccupation. For those who are more experienced, the opportunity to help others not only continues to draw them away from self, but also solidifies and reinforces their own mastery, as they demonstrate to others and as they witness the dramatic changes in the lives and feelings of those others as well as themselves.

Extro • Dynamics is based on natural processes of sharing feelings with others. In order to master it, we must use those processes of sharing for feedback, insights and reinforcement beyond what an individual can achieve independently.

The same concept of people helping each other used so successfully in Alcoholics Anonymous and many other self-help or therapy groups for overcoming behavioral disorders can also be used to achieve lifestyle goals. (One of the reasons there are so many self-help groups is that there are so many kinds of problems — and self-help groups really do help people achieve success in solving problems.)

While individuals may sometimes wish to get together specifically for this process, forming new organizations and groups is not the only answer. The underlying principles and lifestyle techniques of Extro • Dynamics are fundamental to many other processes of interaction. They are consistent with the objectives of other self-help groups, therapy groups, community action services, social agencies, counseling programs, churches, schools and other organizations which seek to develop human potential in group settings or individual treatment. Such groups might easily incorporate the skills and values of Extro • Dynamics into their existing activities.

Our commitment to new lifestyle habits is not a one-time thing. We need the ongoing reinforcement of feedback from others and a regular re-dedication to keeping up lifestyle values and habits. Once we get turned on and all fired up, we need to have some way of keeping the enthusiasm alive when all the negative influences in the world around us work to discourage our idealism. Zig Ziglar, one of the nation's premier motivational speakers, was once asked by an interviewer how effective he thought his motivational workshops really were. The reporter conceded that people at the workshop left in a high state of enthusiasm, ready to "conquer the world," but wondered about the long-term effects — how much of this enthusiasm did they retain days, weeks or months after they finished the workshops. Ziglar noted that bathing and eating are also highly recommended, but you don't just do it one time only. If the participants integrate his program into their daily lives and *really keep their motivation charged up with regular reinforcement,* the enthusiasm will remain. But if it's just a one-time thing, the fire will soon die out and they'll be just like they were before. Ziglar stresses that motivation is not permanent. Neither is bathing or eating. We must keep the mind and body and spirit nourished *on an ongoing basis* [Ziglar 1990].

Go for it! Develop the happiness habit, by setting up your own ongoing practice routines and by working with others.

Other Examples

Conari Press, of Berkeley, California, has published several small volumes entitled *Random Acts of Kindness* and *More Random Acts of Kindness,* which offer numerous examples of "random" acts of cheerful goodwill to those we do not know, with no expectation of anything in return [Conari Press, 1993, 1994]. It is helpful to look for such examples, which not only give us ideas of the kinds of things we can do, but also encourage the desire to put these ideas into practice. I strongly recommend such material!

Observing other models of successful compassionate can not only be motivational, but also instructional. Reading about others who have found joy and peace through their kindness towards others (or their freedom from bitterness upon forgiving those who

73

have caused them pain), can not only inspire us to follow the same path, but to show not only that it is possible, but how others have done it. The television show *"What Would You Do?,"* hosted by Jon Quiñones, shows examples of those who act compassionately as well as those who do not, and the consequences of either choice.

Overcoming Resistance

In adopting Extro • Dynamics as an ongoing behavioral model, there are three phases we go through: 1) Acceptance of the *idea* of Extro • Dynamics, and understanding that there is a difference between accepting the *ideas* or *values,* and applying it as an internalized *habit;* 2) Overcoming the initial resistance to actually getting started in Extro • Dynamics; 3) Developing the initial, forced practice into an automatic and ongoing part of everyday activities.

Acquiring Extro • Dynamics as an automatic habit is similar to learning any new skill, whether it's tying our shoes, learning a language, typing, or an athletic skill such as gymnastics.

Consider the skill of tying shoes. Little babies don't understand anything about wearing shoes, much less tying them. At some point they become aware that someone puts these things on their feet and ties them. They understand that the skill exists, but they don't know how to do it. When they're ready to learn the skill, someone slowly, carefully, shows them how to tie their shoes. They try it themselves. Carefully, awkwardly, and *it doesn't work.* They practice and they try. They practice and they try. Slowly, they get to the point where they can perform the skill, but with a great deal of conscious, difficult effort. Even the early *successes* are awkward. But with sufficient repetitions, it becomes smooth and easy. After a while, they tie their shoes without even thinking about it, and they come to think of it as a childishly simple task.

It's similar to learning to use a computer, or driving a stick shift. The first time you try to drive a stick, you let out the clutch and the car jerks forward. It's very awkward. It's very difficult. Maybe you kill the engine and you have to start over, and try again — but with sufficient practice you get to the point where you slide into the driver's seat, let out the clutch, and off you go. Very smooth, very easy — you do it without even thinking about it.

As we look over our schedules and set aside the times to practice the techniques, we also need to look at the situations in which we will have to implement the model. Not all situations are the same. And the question often comes up, particularly in regard to situations in which it is very difficult to feel warmly towards people who are malicious or annoying:

Can a model based on compassion really be practical and realistic in day-to-day affairs? Can we really apply Extro • Dynamics *universally*, in *every encounter?*

There are, of course, many obstacles in applying Extro • Dynamics universally — in *every* encounter. Some people make it harder to draw out feelings of value than others. During moments of unpleasant interpersonal friction, compassionate feelings may be more difficult. Sometimes you may not even want to try. The objection has been raised several times: "Every time I try to be the 'nice guy,' I end up getting taken advantage of." Or they'll drag out the old quote, "Nice guys finish last."

Is this realistic?

Is Extro • Dynamics really practical in day-to-day affairs?

When desires, goals and values work together harmoniously instead of against each other, life operates more smoothly, and we are able to achieve more of our goals, enjoy more of your desires and get along with others w.

Personal empowerment: Compassion is not weakness. Bullies and those who seek to dominate others do not act out of strength, but rather out of their insecurities. Persons of strength feel empowered to treat others well, and know that this not only makes interpersonal interactions more pleasant, but also empowers greater success in achieving desired social outcomes.

As told in a famous fable of Æsop, a cold north wind, no matter how hard it blows, cannot force the coat off a winter traveler. But the sun radiates a gentle warmth that persuades him to take it off of his own volition.

Public policy empowerment: At the level of public policy, conciliation, nonviolence and bringing people together is far more successful in achieving desired outcomes, even against astronomical odds, in overcoming difficult challenges.

By repaying violent hatred with grieving but loving forgiveness, these families join other moral giants such as Mohandas K. Gandhi, Martin Luther King, Jr. and Nelson Mandela as symbols of heroism who demonstrate exactly why compassionate nonviolence is not only morally superior but more successful in achieving challenging outcomes than its less inspiring alternatives.

If Mahatma Gandhi had rebelled against the British Empire by raising armed rebellion and seeking overthrow by force, he would have been quickly crushed. But by eschewing force and, instead, rising up with nonviolent direct action, the power of moral authority he engendered brought down the greatest empire in the history of the world, on which the sun never set. This action set in motion the liberation of Britain's other colonies along with those of other nations. Gandhi not only brought down empires, he transformed "imperialism" from a title of honor to an epithet of shame.

If Dr. King had led riots and tried to engage in violent reaction to the powers of Southern racial oppression, he would have been just one more rioter removed from the streets and forgotten. Instead, having read the words of Gandhi, and as a follower of a pacifist view of Jesus, King used the transformative moral power of nonviolent direct action and brought down a system of race-based oppression that had persisted for centuries.

President Mandela started out as a sometimes violent and militant political activist against the South African system of institutionalized racism known as apartheid. Such strategies, however justifiable by the evils they sought to remediate, changed nothing. It resulted only in a lengthy prison sentence, however unjust, while the oppression continued. In prison, however, Mandela read of the words and works of Gandhi and King, welcomed them deep into his heart and, in becoming one of them, was able to radiate the moral persuasion to emerge from his cell and lead his nation to a peaceful and nonviolent overthrow of centuries of race-based domination to such an extent of compassion and forgiveness that his Truth and Reconciliation commissions brought healing and unity that had previously been seen as impossible.

The survivors and families of Mother Emanuel AME Church of Charleston, South Carolina, faced unspeakable tragedy and deep personal loss perpetrated with evil and malicious intent. They responded — in the depths of their own intense and unimaginable grieving — with love, compassion and forgiveness that moved the world and inspired all but the most intransigent to join them in calling for a removal of all symbols of armed rebellion against the United States and resistance to human rights struggles. Those who just weeks earlier could never have imagined voting to remove the Confederate battle flag, a symbol that had flown over the statehouse grounds for more than fifty years in protest against civil rights gains, came together in almost complete unanimity to take down that symbol of rebellion and oppression. Many whose hearts were changed explicitly cited the moral power of the survivors' and relatives' compassionate forgiveness in explaining their conversions. If the Charleston families had responded to the hate-fueled massacre with looting and violence, it would have been just one more riot and nothing would have changed. But in repaying hateful violence with love, forgiveness and calls for unity, even some of the hardest hearts were softened and the flag came down.

So the answer to the question of whether or not such a lifestyle is practical or realistic is an unqualified "Yes!" Not only does Extro • Dynamics improve every situation, but in the most challenging of them, its ability to reverse unpleasant feelings of friction and tension, and turn them into happy feelings of compassionate joy, is one of its most important benefits. Situations of extreme adversity may not be the best place for beginners to start. In the long run, however, these will provide the greatest opportunity for satisfaction. We'll show some real life examples in the next chapter.

Chapter 5 Summary
Understanding Extro • Dynamics as an idea or concept will not make it work until we overcome the resistance to change comfortable (but unproductive) old habits, and let the four simple steps become a new and habitual part of our everyday lives.

Lifestyle Situations

Our encounters with other people fit into three basic categories: **Positive relationships**, such as with romantic partners, business associates, friends and many relatives; **Neutral interactions**, as with strangers or casual encounters; and **Negative interactions**, such as those with enemies, competitors, or people who intrude into our lives or harass us. There is also a fourth category, a special way in which Extro • Dynamics can reverse negative conditions in our lives: **crisis** — *acute* self-preoccupation arising from more extreme conditions of intense anxiety, tension, stress or pressure.

Let's examine each of these in greater detail:

Positive Relationships

At first it might seem that positive relationships should be the easiest in which to incorporate Extro • Dynamics. Perhaps it is true that the climate of favorable association and common interests may encourage the positive sharing of Extro • Dynamics.

However, most kinds of positive relationships include a strong built-in factor of *expectation* of something from the other person, which is often the basis for the relationship. It is more akin to *cooperation,* the process of give-and-take, than Extro • Dynamics. Extro • Dynamics is something different: contributing to someone else, from *their* point of view, *without expecting anything in return*. Extro • Dynamics *can* be added to such relationships, but it is not automatically there. It must be specifically and separately added, through each step of the model, up to what we actually *do*

— anything *beyond* what would be expected from the nature of the association.

Dr. Leo Buscaglia notes that, "Mature intimacy and love are not based upon expectations. Since no one, not even a saint, can know or meet all of our expectations, to expect from others is to court pain and disappointment." [Buscaglia 1972, p. 128]

Look over your lifestyle. Identify positive relationships or interactions from which you expect something in return, such as relatives, romantic partners, business associates, and friends. Here are some examples of ways in which Extro • Dynamics can enhance these interactions:

Family situations. Again, domestic interactions include the strong built-in factor of *expectation* from the other person, which is often central to the relationship itself. We have certain expectations from a spouse or lover, and we expect certain things from our children. But we can still go through each step of selfless direction, up to and including an appropriate cheerful contribution of behavior. Perhaps a special gift, or an unexpected surprise, or little notes left around to express appreciation, or even helping someone through a difficult time. But whatever it is, it has to be something *beyond* what would normally be expected from the nature of the association, and it has to be *from the viewpoint of the other person* — not what you think *should be* in their best interests. If your focus is truly directed toward the *other person's perspective,* you will automatically and spontaneously enjoy the process of making special contributions, beyond mutual expectations, from that person's actual frame of reference.

Domestic Relations. Husbands — do you give yourself to your wife just because of what you expect in return? Are you sensitive to experiences as *she* sees them, hears them, smells them or touches them?

Wives — do you look at the disagreements you have with your husband from *his* point of view — the way he sees them, hears them, smells them or touches them?

Have you ever considered what it is like — *really like* — to be married to yourself? How does your spouse see you, *from their perspective,* as you walk into the room? How does your spouse hear your words as you speak them? If we can listen to the words we speak *as others hear them,* we may soon begin to choose those words very differently.

How do parents look, sound, feel to our children? What does the world look like from their smaller perspective? How does the world feel from their viewpoint of limited experience?

Employer—Employee. Instead of looking at those we work with as competitors for limited financial "spoils," we become aware that much of our waking hours are spent in the company of co-workers — often one of the richest resources of human value. We can find many little ways in which to brighten the lives and feelings of those around us, and make a cheerful contribution so the workplace becomes a happier place for all. Not only from an unselfish standpoint, but by seeking ways to enrich the lives and feelings of others, and always doing more than agreed upon (either as employers or employees), we also become more valuable to those who share our economic environment, and thus more valuable in terms of our own opportunities to advance. The employer who always offers a little more, who is cheerful, who finds constructive ways to motivate, who *understands* his *employees'* perspectives, will always be appreciated and respected, and will find that happy, confident employees are more productive. The employee who always works a little longer, is a little more accurate, and does a little extra will always be the most valuable. Is this practical in the real business world? Bob Basso, Ph.D., whose positive approach to management success has been profiled by *People* magazine[1], has made a career out of teaching employers and employees how to *increase productivity* and *fatten the bottom line* by working together towards common goals in a process of "Light Management" — while enjoying a more cheerful work environment in the process [Basso & Klosek].

Landlord—Tenant. Landlords and tenants often become adversaries with seemingly opposing interests. Renters are protective of their home and family environment, and landlords want to safeguard their expense, high-risk investment. Again, those who

---

[1]*People* magazine, September 19, 1983.

always contribute just a little more than expected (whether landlord or tenant) and respond to the needs and feelings of the other from *their* perspectives, will also receive benefits beyond their unselfish motives. Landlords who are quick to make repairs, who keep rental costs as reasonable as possible while still earning a fair return on investment, and who are cheerful will find that they are able to attract and keep the best tenants. The cheerful environment will minimize "nuisance" requests. Tenants who pay rent promptly, take care of the property, and always find *extra* ways to contribute to the well-being of the property and of other tenants, will be appreciated by those to whom rents are paid. They will be able to maximize whatever flexibility is available from this particular landlord to create the most favorable rental conditions.

Seller—Buyer. Sellers often perceive buyers as people with money up for grabs. Buyers often perceive sellers as those who are trying to take as much of their money as possible while doing as little as possible in exchange. Those offering goods or services for sale should visualize approaching customers as fellow human beings who need what they're selling. They should do everything possible to enjoy the process of contributing to the well-being and happiness of those customers, always making sure that something more than agreed upon is added to each transaction. Such merchants will find themselves in great demand by customers, resulting in increased success of their business operations. Conversely, customers approaching merchants should be aware of the busy schedules and other pressures on those they do business with, and find ways to make it as easy and convenient as possible for merchants to serve them. Such an approach would make it easier to receive greater quality and service from more contented merchants.

Of course, in each of these situations *(domestic relations, employer-employee, landlord-tenant, or seller-buyer)* Extro • Dynamics is no guarantee that because you are good to others that they will be good to you, but it will encourage the best possible response. Remember, your intention in true Extro • Dynamics is not to get a better response; if so, then the attention is not really focused away from self *without expectation*. Using Extro • Dynamics, you can truly focus your attention towards the interests of someone other than yourself. But, paradoxically, an improved response is an extra by-product that often results. (For more on how this works, see the section on "Getting What You Want.") Most important is that those who make these extra contributions to others will find themselves operating in a happier, more cheerful environment.

Neutral interactions

In neutral encounters such as crowds or in passing strangers on the street, there are not really any built-in incentives nor obstacles to doing it. Each new interaction, if it is neutral, by its very nature begins with a "clean slate." However, it is easy to pass up the fleeting opportunities for interaction that appear so subtlety and vanish so quickly. But developing Extro • Dynamics in such encounters opens up vast new potentials for enjoying previously overlooked human value — going through each step of the model, ending with a cheerful contribution.

Such interactions may be individual efforts or organized volunteer activities. Contributing to neutral interactions might be nothing more than sharing a pleasant greeting with someone we pass on the street or changing a flat tire for a stranded driver. In each case we open ourselves up to the unlimited opportunities around us. A brief encounter may blossom into real friendship. In fact, our friends were, at one time, strangers.

Some of my most rewarding experiences have involved people I didn't know. Early in life I learned to speak Spanish as well as the American Sign Language used by Deaf people. When I was in my early twenties, I spent a number of Sunday afternoons at Pilgrim Towers in Los Angeles, a retirement home for elderly deaf people run by the Lutheran Church. I would spend several hours talking and listening to wonderful old people's stories from the past, and gaining new insights into the history of Deaf culture and a different perspective on American history. If my friends enjoyed our visits, it could only be a small fraction as much as I did.

Similarly, I have gone to shelters for homeless Spanish-speaking immigrants, and enjoyed meeting new friends and sharing insights of international culture and history that I would have otherwise missed if I had overlooked the value in these strangers.

Those who spend a few hours of their Thanksgiving or Christmas serving strangers at homeless shelters or rescue missions find a deeper enjoyment and meaning to their holidays and radiate a special glow of joy and satisfaction when they join their families and other loved ones. Those who share the joy of strangers pay a very small price to find a very great treasure.

Sharing the joy of neutral interactions doesn't just mean helping those in distress. It may mean enjoying cheerfulness instead of enduring unpleasantness in a crowd or line, or finding creative ways to enjoy our time in traffic. On my car, I have bumper sticker that says, "Practice Random Kindness…," inspired by a slogan attributed to Anne Herbert. The enjoyment of "random kindness" spreads cheerful good joy to all those around, but to none more than those who express themselves in kindness. Conari Press, of Berkeley, California, has published a couple of small volumes which offer great suggestions and examples of random kindness in "neutral" interactions that not only present ideas of what we can do, but also inspire and motivate us to do it [Conari Press, 1993, 1994].[1]

We are surrounded by countless opportunities to expand our interactions with others. Why should we limit those opportunities only to the people we already know?

Negative Relationships
At first glance, negative relationships do not seem to include any built-in factors to facilitate Extro • Dynamics. But, while hostile circumstances may not be the place to *begin* in early practicing, Extro • Dynamics *does work in such situations*. In fact, possibly one of its greatest benefits is its ability to turn conflicts into constructive, positive exchanges.

At a simple level of reversing petty annoyances, it is easy to see how this works. One afternoon, I was working quietly at my desk when I heard a commotion outside. I went to the door to see what was going on. Two young boys were playing baseball in the street a few doors down, using a hardball. I watched as the neighbor

---

[1]Conari Press encourages participation in random kindness, and will provide free assistance and information towards that goal. They can be reached at 1144 65th Street, Suite B, Emeryville, California 94608.

whose house they were in front of came storming angrily out. "What do you think you're doing?" he yelled. "Don't play baseball here. You're going to break a window in someone's house or damage someone's car!" And he stormed back into his house. The boys didn't stop playing, they just moved down the street in front of another house. I watched as *that* neighbor came out of his house. He went over to the boys, smiled, and said, "I didn't know you guys liked to play baseball! I used to play ball in high school. Hold on a sec, let me show you something." He went into his house and came out again, holding some baseballs. "Look at this…" It was a baseball signed by various members of the Los Angeles Dodgers. He also showed them a small bag of baseballs. "These are official National League baseballs, the kind they use in the Major Leagues. That's the kind I like to play with — the best! I don't get much chance to play as often as I'd like. I remember once when I was young, playing ball in the street and, *whack!* I creamed one — right through my neighbor's window. Boy, was I scared. So, maybe this isn't the best place to play ball, but, I'll tell you what, I'll be through with what I'm doing in about an hour. Would you guys like to go with me to the park and hit a few?" This neighbor saw the world from the children's point of view, and was able to find a cheerful way to solve the problem. I considered how easy it is to reverse unpleasant feelings, yet how few people do it.

Here's another example of how one man did it on a small scale:

Newspaper columnist Sydney J. Harris relates the following experience of how he and a friend stopped at a newsstand to purchase a paper one evening. His friend graciously thanked the vendor, who remained coldly silent. "A sullen fellow, isn't he?" remarked Harris afterward, as they continued along their way.

"Oh, he's that way every night," said the friend.

"Then why do you continue to be so very polite to him?" asked Harris.

His friend responded with, "Why should I let *him* decide how *I'm* going to act?" [Harris p. 94]

Similarly, in an oft-repeated story President Abraham Lincoln was criticized for rewarding his political enemies with appointments to key positions. He responded with, "Do I not destroy an enemy when I make him a friend?" If we can respond to strangers or enemies the way we would if the same behavior was committed by a loved one, we can destroy enmity by turning it into friendship.

It is necessary to make the distinction between *persons* and *behaviors*. Unconditional love of the person does not require acceptance of behaviors which are wrong or which cause harm.

That's easy to *say,* but how do we *do* it?

Beyond just saying, "love your enemies" we need to know *how.* *How* do you enjoy happy feelings of compassionate love when someone cuts you off in traffic, or pulls a gun and steals your wallet? Is this realistic? We need to know *how* to treat others compassionately without becoming doormats!

People often say to me, "Every time I try to be compassionate, other people take advantage of me." There is a difference between *unconditional love* and *unconditional acceptance.* Compassion can never be equated with weakness. *It is not an act of compassion to allow others to do things that hurt themselves and others.* In fact, true love and concern will motivate you to help others overcome destructive or co-dependent behaviors and build the personal self-worth that renders these counterproductive outlooks obsolete. Dr. Scott Peck emphasizes at great length that such pathological dependency is not a sign of real love, but the enemy of true love [Peck, pp. 98-105 and pp. 160-169].

The key is to *make sure you go through all four of the steps.* Just as some people get stuck on the first step, focusing on their own needs and nothing else, locking themselves in prisons of self-preoccupation, others skip over the first step (their own innate worth) and the second step (neutral, equal recognition of all participants) and devote their energies exclusively to the third step: recognizing the importance of other people. They become doormats. They become excessively dependent. They focus on other people and nothing else. In cases where this destruction to self-esteem is forcibly and externally imposed, as in the case of kidnapping, hostage-taking or abuse of women, we observe the otherwise inexplicable phenomenon in which the natural process of empathetic bonding causes victims to bond with those who cause their suffering — hostages become loyal to their captors (the

"Stockholm Syndrome") [Roan in *Los Angeles Times*, 8-20-91, p. E-5], and women refuse to leave their abusers.

Such a perspective is just as destructive as a purely self-directed one. Use *all* of the steps! Appreciate and celebrate your own unique personal value and take care of basic personal needs. If you have self-respect and self-esteem, you will not permit others to trample over your needs and feelings. But don't stop there! Go on to the second step: break free of the prison of self-centered preoccupation, and move to the third step: celebrate and enjoy the value of another human being with a merging and combining of their value *with yours,* and keep going: take *action* to make a specific, joyful contribution that is really in the best interests of each unique individual involved.

You can have compassion and caring, even for a person who is vicious or nasty, without accepting the undesirable behavior itself and, in fact, actively opposing behavior that is harmful to themselves or others.

For example, we often hear that we should feel compassion for *victims* rather than *criminals*. Let's look at a victim who is easy to share feelings with. What about a child? One of the projects we have been involved with is for children who have been removed from their homes due to physical, emotional or sexual abuse. Some of these kids have been through horrible things, beyond what most grownups could ever imagine. At the sight of a four-year-old child who has been physically beaten and emotionally abused, we want to take him in our arms and hug him and tell him everything will be okay and find a better place to put him where he can be nurtured and taken care of so no one will ever mistreat him again.

But what about when we fail? What about a kid we never find — never get a chance to help? We don't find him at age four. Instead we find him twenty years later, at age twenty-four. We find him when he's breaking into our car or robbing us on the street. Remember, he's the kid we *didn't* help. Same kid, but now he's not so cute or adorable. All he's learned is cruelty and violence. You talk about compassion for *victims* instead of *criminals?* Our prisons are filled with victims — the ones who *didn't* get help.

Our response can and should be one of understanding and compassion. Our goal should not be to punish but to provide the nurturing and good experiences they never had. Even if they steal our property, we need not let them also rob us of compassion and replace it with fear or anger.

That doesn't excuse their behavior. We still have to stop harmful behavior — forcefully if necessary. One person suggested to me that the "compassionate" way to respond to a street robber who steals your wallet would be to offer him your watch as well. That misses the point. Is it an act of compassion to let someone go on doing things that hurt others and hurt themselves, too? No. Sometimes we have to say, "No!" Just like parents. We love our kids. But even when we have to discipline them with firmness, we don't stop loving them.

Even when the negative condition itself cannot be eliminated (we still cannot control others, nor does this model even suggest any expectation of something from them), the change in our perspective, because we are directed away from self-concern, makes us less susceptible to hurt. Because we are not preoccupied with our own suffering, we have fewer negative feelings. We can respond with understanding and goodwill. Our happy feelings minimize their ability to hurt us or "get to" us.

Becoming directed away from self allows the possibility of seeing familiar issues through a different perspective. What are the usual feelings about someone who is a liar, thief and cheat? How can these attributes be viewed differently? Perhaps a perspective that is more constructive and more objective can allow more depth to be seen in multiple dimensions. Perhaps it may be possible to perceive the creativity, flexibility and determination to survive that are represented in these traits. Perhaps the *real* truth might also be seen — that these evils mask not only talents, but also conceal the underlying *fears* of frightened, insecure children whose fundamental human needs have never been met, or they wouldn't be wallowing in behaviors that hurt themselves, hurt others and do nothing good for anyone. This is not to *accept* the evil. It is to *understand* it more comprehensively, and to see the real path toward defeating it.

When you are directed away from your preoccupation with yourself, you become less sensitive to pain that others can inflict on you. And when that selfless direction is focused on another person — especially the person causing the pain — you can go through each of the steps carefully, and develop an appreciation and love for that person (apart from the person's *behavior*) which is a positive and gentle feeling, and which minimizes the anger or hurt the person can cause. You can enjoy the benefit of interacting with that person, *with or without* their knowledge or consent — *even if they intend to cause the opposite!*

Extro • Dynamics is an *active process*. It is not a matter of being sort of vaguely directed in a selfless direction. It is a specific and attentive focusing toward another person, going through each of the steps, to draw out the *value* that can be internalized from those who are negative. In drawing out that value, their power to impose negative feelings on you is eliminated.

Extro • Dynamics lets you rescind the power of others over your feelings. You can take your own direct positive action, becoming free from unpleasant negative reactions. In the words of "Dear Abby," [Column dated 2-21-89] "To forgive is to set a prisoner free, and discovering that the prisoner was *you.*" In the poem, "Forgiveness," George Roemisch describes forgiveness as "the fragrance of the violet which still clings fast to the heel that crushed it." [Quoted by Dear Abby 2-5-96]

We can also identify specific individuals for whom we have negative feelings: perhaps a person who has cheated us in business; perhaps a lover who has betrayed us; perhaps a person who was responsible for a violent or cruel act that caused us or our loved ones to suffer.

Note of caution to protect self and others: Especially in situations where serious economic or emotional or physical harm has been caused to ourselves or others, we do not need to accept or embrace the wrong *behavior*. We need to differentiate between the *person* and the *behavior*. In such situations of serious harm, *to protect ourselves **and others** from very real threats of harm or the continuation of real harm, we may need to take aggressive action to ensure that such harmful, damaging behavior is stopped and* *that the person is not able to continue it.* But we can understand and accept the *person* so that our negative response will be reversed and that we curtail the consequential negative feelings such as anger, jealously and bitterness, that poison our own souls and perpetuate and magnify the suffering for ourselves, while doing nothing to punish the guilty party or curtail their harmful behavior. If such situations have to be faced on a regular basis, we can make mental and emotional preparations to deal with them in advance. By being prepared, we can act in accordance with pre-formulated plans rather than in the pressure of heated emotional feelings as they erupt.

Where necessary, restructure lifestyle patterns, or change those situations by removing yourself from the sources of stress and pres-sure that draw your attention toward self. Eliminate those conditions of frustration, aggravation, or pain!

Still, it is not possible to avoid all negative situations. For those that cannot be eliminated, Extro • Dynamics can minimize the negative reactions to those interpersonal frictions. And, when we can't handle a particularly troublesome situation, professional help or group feedback may be needed to move away from self-directed obsessions.

Paradoxically, when you look through the perspective of your adversary, not only do you reduce their ability to hurt you, but because you see *their* point of view, you also may gain insight into the most effective approach for getting through to them, and improve whatever chance you might have had of solving the underlying problem as well (although that reciprocal benefit is a separate issue from Extro • Dynamics).

Many negative situations erupt suddenly. There is no time to prepare for them. But if we have mastered Extro • Dynamics in less challenging situations, we can move rapidly through the first three steps, always ready for unpredictable negative situations.

In situations where we *do* have some reason to suspect in advance that there may be some interpersonal friction, prepare yourself by visualizing the ways in which you can draw Extro • Dynamics into the situation. By planning in advance the kind of response you will make, you can remain in control of your feelings and continue reaching away from self, without letting someone else force your attention toward self-preoccupation.

Again, whether or not you are able to *change* their behavior is not the issue. You may try, and you may succeed or you may not be able to change it at all. But no matter what happens, their behavior will not be able to get to you and hurt you as long as your feelings are directed away from self-preoccupation.

Such situations might include: tensions of stop-and-go rush-hour traffic; pressures from people or situations in your work environment; domestic tensions; relationships or interactions with those individuals who cause you pain — use the value of their personal resources to neutralize their ability to hurt you.

For example: in domestic situations, perhaps you are coming home from work and, as you pull into the garage, you realize that your spot is blocked by the laundry basket because your spouse is doing the laundry and wasn't careful about where she or he set the basket down while the wash was running. A trivial thing — but *it's the third time this week the same thing has happened!* And you have already made it clear just how much this annoys you. How do you respond? I asked this question in a workshop. One person suggested that, in order to avoid being taken advantage of, it is now time to be assertive. It is time to act firmly, but without losing concern and caring for the person.

Okay — it's time for direct action. I believe in being assertive. And the time is *now*. If you put it off, the annoyance will just fester and eventually erupt as something more than it really has to be. But our action must be not only with "concern" and "caring" but with awareness of *the viewpoint of the other person*. If a husband just storms into the house and shouts, "Goddammit! You left your damn laundry basket in my parking space again for the third time this week!" all he's likely to get is a big fight.

"Oh yeah! Well, at least I'm *doing* the laundry. I work eight hours every day, too, and when I get home I still have to make dinner, clean the house and do your damn laundry while you sit around watching TV. Why don't *you* ever do the laundry?!"

On the other hand, if the husband, upon arriving home and having to get out of his car and move the basket, would approach the situation using Extro • Dynamics, he could be firm and assertive, but with a very different response.

He could first re-affirm his own special importance, and that the emotional intensity of his reaction (anger) validates him as a person of deep feelings. Then, by reaching away from self to a neutral perspective and viewing the situation objectively, he can move into the visual and emotional perspective from his wife's point of view. In addition to identifying with general sensory perceptions from her perspective, more specifically he can visualize what it must like to work eight hours, then come home and do the laundry while fixing dinner for a husband who sits around and does nothing. Such a perspective may allow him to face the issue before his wife raises it in anger and defensiveness.

This may cause the husband to have a different reaction. First of all, reaching away from self and through a perspective of another human being will diffuse his anger completely. (It may even replace it with a little guilt, but that would draw the perspective back to self — better to retain a selfless viewpoint and consider constructive behavioral responses.) Second, he may conclude that the best response, which such a perspective will almost automatically lead to, is to determine what *action* he can contribute to her experience. He may no longer feel like saying anything at all, and just move the laundry basket himself while also figuring out how to make a more equitable contribution to existing household chores.

If the husband still feels that, in addition to finding better ways to contribute to household chores, he also needs to remind his wife about the careless placement of the laundry basket, this selfless perspective will certainly cause him to express his message in a more positive form. Perhaps something like, "Hi honey, on my way home from work I couldn't help but think of all the things you do for me around here, even after you've been working all day, and how much I appreciate it. Then, when I pulled into the garage and saw the laundry basket there, instead of getting mad again, it seemed so trivial compared to all you do that I just moved it myself. I'm really amazed at how much you're able to do, and I realized that I need to do more around the house myself." No anger. No fight. And a much greater likelihood that, next time his wife does the laundry she will *want* to be more thoughtful about where she leaves the basket. And, in the spirit of *action,* the husband may be motivated to actually pitch in and do something to help with household responsibilities.

Another example: if you're driving down the freeway and a stranger (or worse, a "freeway competitor") cuts in front of you, your first response might be one of anger. But what if you were driving in caravan with your brother, your best friend and your boss, and one of *them* cut you off? Or tailgated you? Or did something else that was rude or dangerous? Would you blow your top and make an obscene gesture? If it were serious enough, you may take action to remedy a dangerous situation, but your response would probably be constructive and positive. Extro • Dynamics turn strangers into friends, and lets us respond accordingly.

If traffic is one of *your* problems, as it was mine for a long time, prepare for it as soon as you get in your car. Remind yourself that some time during this trip, there is a good chance someone might do something rude or dangerous. It may be a person who is otherwise very good and kind in a brief moment of carelessness or thoughtlessness. Also remember that *most* of the drivers you encounter will be following the rules and acting thoughtfully and courteously. Then, as you drive, look around and see the hundreds of cars you normally ignore because they aren't doing anything wrong, and notice how rare it is that someone does act badly. When that rare bad moments finally comes up, instead of being shocked and outraged, you can easily dismiss it as the rarity that it is, balanced by the overwhelming preponderance of good drivers, and by drawing yourself into the value of that person and finding a pleasant or understanding response to defuse the situation.

Similarly, at the start of each trip, decide that you will watch for ways to help other drivers. It is not "giving in" to them — it is refusing to let them have power over your feelings. Affirm your own special value, then look for the same value in each of the many drivers you will encounter. Experience the situation selflessly, through *their* perspectives. Re-read the detailed example of the steps at the beginning of Chapter 5, which uses the model of a situation in traffic.

Even if their behavior is rude or incompetent, think of the many reasons *why* good people do wrong things. Perhaps they are late or rushing to handle an emergency (when has that caused *you* to do something rude or careless, even though not maliciously?); or perhaps they are less experienced drivers than you; or perhaps they are lost travelers in a strange place. Even if they are just downright mean, consider the factors that can cause people to become malicious: pressures they can't quite cope with; deprivations or abuse they grew up with, causing them to function at a lower level of interaction than you do. (If it appears that the streets are full of drivers who are less competent than you are or whose personal values are inferior to yours, take it as a compliment. But if you are "superior" to someone else, it is only your spirit of compassion that makes you so. If, in your frustration, you become as rude or angry as they are, you are no longer superior.) You don't know *why* they are this way, but there must be something wrong, because healthy, well-adjusted people don't do things that are unpleasant for themselves and others. As mentioned earlier, Extro • Dynamics will not make you a mind reader, but if you look through a selfless perspective you will easily find many reasons to explain (not justify) another person's inappropriate behavior. You can draw on the inherent value in each of the other "faceless," impersonal drivers around you, *especially* the rude ones. This perspective will cause you to naturally *do* the things that will make the traffic situation you share one that is more pleasant for them ... and for *you!*

If you find it difficult to remember this in advance each time you begin a trip, make yourself a note and tape it to your steering wheel to help you remember. In time, it will become your natural, automatic way of responding to a situation that used to cause tension and frustration. It can change your life, as it has mine.

Additionally, use other devices to direct your attention away from self-preoccupation. Listen to self-improvement tapes, or let your mind wander imaginatively to pleasant thoughts and daydreams, as if reclining in a favorite chair. My wife Thelma takes advantage of long drives as "quiet time" when she can relax and sort out her thoughts and ideas.

If this seems too simplistic, just consider: does your way (getting angry and upset) work any better? Use this simple model. You really will feel much better. But it is important to emphasize that you should make the decision to do so as soon as you get in the car. If you feel too much resistance at the start of driving, the resistance will be far stronger when you are already in a state of annoyance.

Sounds good on paper, but is it realistically possible to have good feelings about someone who is trying to hurt you? Yes!

On a day-to-day basis, when the basic skills have been mastered, it may become easy to reverse routine frictions and minor annoyances involving other people. But what about on a larger scale? Could Extro • Dynamics help in coping with major tragedies caused by the malice of others?

No matter what you have gone through or what someone else has done to you, you can reach out to that person and use the value of their uniquely special perspective to take away their power to hurt you.

How about an extreme case? Could survivors of Hitler's holocaust feel compassion toward those who imposed such mindless cruelty on them? At a sufficient level of spiritual attainment, *it can be done.* In fact, there were those who were able to do just that — to face the most awful horrors of personal torture or even death with calm and dignity. No one had the power to take that away from them as long as their perspectives were directed away from self. The psychotherapist Dr. Viktor Frankl was himself a prisoner in the Nazi concentration camps yet, in his book, *Man's Search for Meaning,* he relates that there were those rare individuals who "...walked through the huts comforting others, giving away their last piece of bread. They may have been few in number, but they offer sufficient proof that everything can be taken from a man but one thing: the last of the human freedoms — to choose one's attitude in any given set of circumstances...." [Frankl p. 75] Understandably, few who were subjected to that cruelty were able to respond this way. For most people, part of their victimization is the impairment of their sensitivity and compassion. But it *can* be done! And there were, in fact, many who faced torture and death with dignity and compassion, achieving a deep con-tent-ment that no one could take from them.

Could someone really do that?

Over the years I have accumulated a collection of stories, clipped from newspapers, magazines, etc. They are all *true* stores, about real people who used the personal value of adversaries to enrich their own lives, under conditions far beyond what most of us would ever have to face.

There is one about a man who was shot in the head by a robber, and badly traumatized, both physically and emotionally. After an initial and understandable response of anger, fear and bitterness, he eventually found that the only way he could put an end to his suffering, and end the robber's hold over his life, was to reach out to his attacker. He wrote a letter to the attacker, met him in prison, and developed a long and close friendship even after the robber had finished his time in prison. He was not only able to end his own torment and bitterness resulting from that horrible attack, but he was also able to find the special value in this vicious attacker, to transform the life of his assailant, and to help him to become a successful and productive human being [Walborn, pp. 16-19].

There are three separate but similar articles about couples whose only sons were killed by drunk drivers. Again, despite understandable initial shock and bitterness, they eventually learned to undo and reverse that bitterness by becoming not only acquaint-ed with, but *close to* the killers of their sons. While they could not undo the tragedy of their losses, they could put an end to the ability of another person to hurt them, and not only put their own lives in order, but also salvage troubled lives badly in need of someone to give them the nurturing that they had never known [Morris, pp. 1-6; Ellerbusch, pp. 27-30 and Boley, pp. 2-5].

There are many such stories. An Irish policeman is assassinated and his widow eventually finds peace by forgiving the IRA terror-ist who killed him [Cobb, pp. 1-6]. Crime victims reach out to those who victimized them [Holbrook, pp. 1-7]. An elderly African-American community leader, victimized by a senseless racially-motivated beating, finds peace through forgiveness of his attackers and helping them to learn tolerance through community service and personal development instead of serving time in prison [Greene, pp. 10-12]. A widowed pediatrician, in horrible grief at the loss of his daughter to a random act of drunken, teen-aged violence, suffers terrible agony from which no comfort can be found until he begins an active participation in programs to help troubled youth, starting with the two who killed his daughter [Upp, pp. 30-33]. Tormented husbands and wives find freedom from self-directed suffering by reaching out selflessly to the ex-spouses who wronged them (or even worse, to the spouses of their ex-spouses) [Considine, pp. 1-4; Gaines, pp. 10-13]. And on and on.

These are not hypothetical cases. Each of these is a true story about a real person, who learned that there was enough suffering just in *sorrow;* it wasn't necessary to add the suffering of *anger* or *bitterness* as well.

Is it realistic? You bet it is! Is it common? Is it easy? No. That's why these people get written up in the papers.

In May of 1981, Pope John Paul II was shot by Mehmet Ali Agca, but survived his wounds. Subsequently, the Pope met with his attacker face to face in prison, shared a tender and compassionate visit, extending his complete forgiveness. Agca, initially hostile and aloof (boycotting his own trial) was profoundly affected by the exchange, resulting in a dramatic personality change.

The Dalai Lama, exiled secular and religious leader of Tibet, thrives in a successful life of compassionate joyfulness despite being ousted from his homeland by Chinese Communists. He is one of those rare persons able to distinguish between persons and behaviors under very extreme conditions. As a Buddhist monk, he teaches love, compassion and forgiveness toward oppressors, while still struggling vigorously and unceasingly against the evil actions of brutality they commit, with "the light of compassion and awareness" as his weapons with which to "dispel the darkness of fear and oppression." [Dalai Lama, p. 263-265]

An extreme example from ancient times:

Two thousand years ago, a simple teacher of love and gentleness, Jesus of Nazareth, also taught that it was possible to love enemies and return good for evil. In his first public teaching (the Sermon on the Mount), he introduced a radical new concept: he said, "love your enemies; turn the other cheek."[New Testament — Matthew 5:38-46 (Chronology is based on sequence of events in the Gospel of Matthew, and may vary from other Gospels.)]

Jesus' *last* teaching in Jerusalem, prior to the last supper and events leading up to the crucifixion and resurrection, was a parable in which he described the final judgment as being based on the way in which we treat those in distress, saying, "Inasmuch as ye have done it unto one of the least of these my brethren, ye have done it unto me." [New Testament — Matthew 25:31-46.]

This was the centerpiece of Jesus' teaching. When asked to identify the *greatest* commandment, he did not introduce something new, but rather — in his role as a Jewish rabbi — quoted from existing Jewish law: he told us to love God and to love our neighbor as ourselves. When asked to clarify, he told the story of the Good Samaritan to illustrate a very broad definition of "neighbor." He taught that this kind of love was the "first and great commandment," on which all others were based. [New Testament — Matthew 22:36-40; Luke 10:25-37][1]

The Missionaries of Charity, founded by Mother Teresa, uniquely combines the two great commandments to "love God" and "love your neighbor as yourself." They show their love of God directly to him, in his "disguise" of poverty, through their compassionate ministry to the "least of these," as the first among their declaration of principles.

Was it realistic? Jesus himself had to put it to the test.

The ancient practice of crucifixion is one of the most cruel means of execution ever devised. It involves stringing the human body up in a position where the person's full weight is supported only by the outstretched arms, and then leaving him to hang like that until the intense pain finally kills him through a slow process of internal suffocation. Even an expert gymnast in top physical condition has only enough strength to withstand the position of a suspended cross for a few moments. But when the body is fastened

---

[1]In these passages, Jesus is quoting from the Old Testament: Deuteronomy 6:5 "...love the Lord thy God with all thine heart..." and Leviticus 19:18 "...love thy neighbor as thyself...", and emphasizing that they are central in importance.

in place with ropes or nails (according to differing local customs), so that it *can't* drop, it lingers in intense pain for two or three hours until it succumbs to an agonizing death.

That was the kind of cruelty that Jesus was forced to endure in his final moments of mortality. To be sure, his execution was a painful event.

He was a sensitive man who watched as one of his most trusted companions betrayed him with a kiss and another denied even knowing him. He was hurriedly tried by despotic officials of the contemporary religious orthodoxy, who made a travesty of justice. He was forced to carry his own heavy cross through a jeering mob so hostile that even his closest associate denied that he even knew him. While other criminals with him were tied to their crosses with ropes as prescribed by Roman law, he was nailed to his cross with spikes driven through his hands and feet. He asked, in his agony, for water, and they gave him a sponge filled with vinegar. He hung on the cross for more than three hours in the painful process of death by crucifixion.

Under such conditions, with physical pain pulling the consciousness toward self-preoccupation, we could certainly understand if the pressures of that agony caused him to erupt in anguish or fury. Yet as a spiritually advanced being, he was able to reach selflessly to those nearby, and direct himself through the value of their perspectives, responding with enough compassion to overcome the self-directed compulsion of his agonizing pain, and pass on in peace.

Moments before his death, at the height of physical agony, he spoke with compassion for his tormentors: "Father, forgive them; for they know not what they do." [New Testament — Luke 23:34]

Jesus had the spiritual skills and tools to remain master of his own feelings despite what any other person did to him. Having achieved this level of spiritual mastery, he would have felt no temptation to respond otherwise.

What You Can Do: A Challenge — Here is a challenge that will test your mastery of Extro • Dynamics. It is something that everyone should eventually be able to do, but many will find

that it is not appropriate as a "beginning" experiment. If you have any reservations, wait until you are more comfortable in less challenging situations, and come back to this one later.

Look over your life and determine the one person who has hurt you the most. It may be an ex-spouse, a former business partner who cheated you, someone who damaged your good name, or even someone who caused a tragic loss through crime or accident.

Think of this person and go through the steps. Understand the person. Understand who they are and where they have come from. Understand how a human being, born as an innocent infant, could grow to do what this person has done to you. Feel yourself releasing the bitterness and hostility which, while it may be justified, only perpetuates suffering. If someone has already hurt you, do not let them continue to hurt you. *Don't accept wrong or hurtful behavior or make excuses for it — make the distinction between the person and the behavior. It is never an act of compassion to support others in hurting themselves or others.*

Continue through this process until you can enjoy warm feelings of compassionate joyfulness toward this individual from the first three steps. You have truly mastered this model when you can progress all the way through the fourth step and find the appropriate behavioral action in which to make a cheerful contribution of specific action for that person.

Again, turning negatives into positives is difficult for many. Perhaps, for some, part of their victimization is the loss of their ability to feel compassion under adversity. But with sincere effort and determination *it can be done!* Many have been able to do it. No matter how much you have been wronged, there is someone who has suffered greater wrongs who has been able to put an end to the control of their tormentor through active, positive, compassionate joy.

The more you have suffered, the more difficult it will be, but the greater serenity and freedom from suffering you will enjoy.

Special situations of acute anxiety

Situations of acute anxiety may include job-related stresses arising out of career or employment responsibilities; financial insecurities

and budget management pressures; anxieties about romantic relationships, breakups, conflicts, insecurities, and so on; pressures
arising out of day-to-day home environment conditions; grief over
loss of a loved one; the acute attention to Self which accompanies
direct physical pain or illness; or even just the combination of a lot
of minor, petty annoyances that seem to build up. These are often
the same anxieties that cause us to cry *"Why me?"* during personal
crises to ourselves or loved ones (See Chapter 4).

These exceptional situations focus a greater intensity of preoccupation with self. Extro • Dynamics is the ideal solution for
breaking out of the stress and pressure of these situations. However, because the grip of self-preoccupation is so strong, it is very
difficult to focus away from self long enough to even begin.

In such cases, it is necessary to take a moment to first confront
the acute anxiety directly. As a *process of feeling,* the anxiety is
difficult to cope with. Stop for a moment, and confront it *mentally*
rather than at the level of feelings. In recognizing and analyzing it
mentally, you can understand it rather than just experience it. Tell
yourself that you have to go through the steps of Extro • Dynamics,
one by one, even though you don't feel like it.

Then, moving into the process of feeling or experience itself,
force yourself to go through each step of Extro • Dynamics very
carefully, in all the detail in which they are described earlier. After
you have mastered the steps and made them part of your personal
habits, it is usually *not* necessary in routine situations to go through
the first three steps in detail, because you can quickly but effectively reaffirm self value, develop a neutral perspective, and merge
your physical and emotional perspective with those around you.
But under the pressure of acute self-preoccupation, that automatic
process may not flow as readily. Instead, it may be necessary to go
through each step, slowly and in full detail, as you did when you
were getting started. The important thing is to become re-directed
away from self.

Focus specifically on others involved in the situation causing
the anxiety, and use the value of their consciousness to help draw
you beyond self-concern. Also direct yourself toward others who
may have similar anxieties, or other anxieties that are greater than

yours. Participation in self-help groups is ideal for this. Everyone has problems, either as temporary acute crises or ongoing conditions that they have to deal with. *Everyone* has said, "Why me?" at one time or another. But they also have happy times. Draw on all the resources of consciousness available at the time when you really need it.

Additionally, in dealing at the level of feeling, use the tools of feeling that Nature has provided for dealing with acute anxiety. If you need to cry, then do so. You will feel better as pent-up anxieties are released through the spilling of tears. Anxiety, tension and nervousness that are kept bottled up inside become self-directed forms of pent-up energy. Release that pent-up energy through jogging, aerobics, or any intense activity that disperses energies. Draw on that energy and re-channel it away from self, toward something constructive that will make you and others feel better.

Remember also that Extro • Dynamics is only one of many valuable tools available. Use other tools of spirituality and religion, meditation, music, reading, or whatever you can to draw yourself away from that intense self-preoccupation. Where needed, also turn to professional help in the fields of mental health, counseling, or self-help groups for assistance in breaking through the barriers.

Putting It All Together

To summarize the process of implementing the simple Extro • Dynamics model into an ongoing lifestyle habit, let us review exactly what to do:

1. Practice the Extro • Dynamics techniques.

   At the end of Chapter 4 is a concise summary of the steps, presented in a box. Make a copy to keep in your purse or wallet; make a copy to keep in your car; make a copy to keep in your desk at work or school. Permission is granted for you to make as many copies of this copyrighted chart as you need for your own personal, non-commercial use, to help remind you of the steps and put them into practice.

2. Review daily activity schedules to determine the times and places in which to consciously begin using the model in real-life situation.
    - Write out a calendar of your week's normal activities, including work, school, regular social activities, as well as times that are not committed.
    - Make notes how you can integrate the model into these activities.
    - Mark your calendar so you won't forget.

    While the first practice attempts may seem forced and awkward, especially in the course of regular activities, with repeated effort they will become natural and automatic, and you will feel yourself becoming happier and more constructive in all your associations with other people in these situations.

3. Arrange to meet with others who are trying to learn and use the model in daily lifestyle situations.
    - Feedback from others will help you smooth out situations in which you seem to find difficulty; sometimes just trying to explain difficulties to someone else will generate the obvious answers for yourself.
    - Helping others overcome obstacles *they* face in following the model will help you to think and act automatically in ways that are consistent with these techniques.

4. Take a "relationship inventory":
    - Review in your mind the key people who influence your life, feelings and daily activities. For help with this, review your schedule of activities (item #2 above) and think of the people involved in your regular daily activities. Also include people you may not see on a regular basis, but who are important in your life.
    - Notice how these people fit into the three relationship types (note, the same person may be either positive or negative, at different times and in different situations):
      a. Positive: Be specific: think of the person's name and relationship — relatives, romantic partners, friends and co-workers or customers at work. Remember the built-in advantages — the pleasantness and favorable association that already exists. Also remember the

b. Negative: again, be specific. Think of the person's name and the nature of your involvement — enemies, competitors, or those who in some way annoy or harass you. Remember the built-in incentive to improve a bad situation and to change bad feelings into good ones. Also keep in mind the built-in obstacles of conflicting interests, bitterness, anger, unpleasantness, fear, etc., depending on the cause of the negativity. Also remember that understanding and accepting the *person,* and *why* they have become the way they are does not require accepting their wrong behavior. Your new insights may or may not provide a solution to the negative condition, but you *can* reverse their ability to hurt *your* feelings.

c. Neutral: include people you pass on your way to work, in traffic, while shopping, or in many other situations where you are surrounded by strangers. It may also include opportunities to donate time to help unknown people in times of adversity. While there are not really any built-in obstacles or advantages, since these people are not previously known to us, there can be a strong incentive to learn how to relate to the many people who often pass in and out of our lives, so that we may always be surrounded by opportunities to enjoy the cheerfulness of Extro • Dynamics.

Add here a fourth situation: Identify those special situations of acute anxiety such as job related stresses, financial insecurities, anxieties about loneliness or difficulties in romance, health problems including pain and illness, loss of a loved one, or the accumulation of many petty annoyances that seem to gang up on you. Identify the individuals and conditions of your specific situation, and use the value of those around you to enjoy "compassionate joy" and draw yourself away from self-preoccupation, to constructive action that can lead to your ability to put an end to your unpleasant feelings.

5. Don't put it off — *Do it **now!***

Chapter 6 Summary
Extro • Dynamics enhances all interpersonal relationships. It expands the happiness of positive relationships. It opens up new horizons in enjoying neutral interactions. And it can reverse the unpleasantness of negative interactions — to defuse hostilities and tensions or even turn them into positive relationships in new and dynamic ways!

Extro • Dynamics — "Achieving Success Through Compassionate Joy" — can be realistically and successfully integrated into the mainstream of your daily lifestyle activities. Practice the techniques, on your own and with others: from appreciation of self-value, to merging the special value in others with that of your own, and finally doing something about it — finding the right behavior in each situation to contribute to sharing happy feelings. Be happy!

Getting What You Want!

Everyone wants to be wealthy, or at least financially secure. Everyone wants to enjoy success in love and romance, or at least a warm and stable relationship. Everyone wants a long and healthy life and they want to feel youthful, energetic and healthy for as long as it continues.

One of the concerns that people often have in seeking the compassionate life is that they will have to sacrifice their desires for getting money, finding love and enjoying physical well-being. This concern is based on a tragic misconception that has caused many to feel they had to choose between their values and desires.

In fact, the opposite is true. A realistic, practical and truly selfless compassion (as described in the preceding section) will promote successes in other areas of life, not work against them. At the same time, it will address the legitimate needs for attending to self described in the first step, which must be met in order to complete all the steps, including the active unselfishness of a fully-implemented Extro•Dynamics lifestyle.

This is not to say that living compassionately will automatically make you rich, popular, or healthy. Unlike happiness itself, which is not tangible and cannot be obtained by direct physical pursuit (as we saw in Chapters 1 and 2), there are certain tangible aspects of money, love and health. These goals are separate from the pursuit of happiness, and there are many separate volumes written to offer suggestions for success in each of these areas. In fact, success at any one of these goals, or all of them, will not even guarantee the enjoyment of happiness. They are simply distinct aspects of our experience. They are different, but not contradictory. Compassionate unselfishness does not undermine these other pursuits. Networking skills, communication skills, customer relations, employee morale and development, getting along with co-

workers — all of these "people skills" will be made more, not less, successful with a lifestyle of practical compassion.

A person who understands the feelings, needs and motivations of co-workers, superiors, clients and even competitors will be more successful in business, not less. A person who can appeal to the needs and feelings of prospective romantic partners will be more successful in attracting romantic love, not less. A person free from self-preoccupation will be more successful in sticking with exercise programs, overcoming diet-wrecking obsessions with food and developing a balanced lifestyle free from stress.

In contrast, some of those who expend the greatest effort in trying to find and impress just the right lover are the ones who suffer the greatest frustration and chronic loneliness. Those who seek wealth through "get-rich-quick" schemes often live from hand to mouth while dreaming of the next big deal. Even if they can put a few extra bucks in their pockets, they're often hiding from unhappy customers, creditors or even the law, so that they never can really enjoy whatever money happens to come their way. Similarly, there are many who put great effort into trying to achieve health through roller-coaster dieting plans, inconsistent exercise regimens, or are so uptight and self-preoccupied about their health that they drive up their blood pressure, may suffer from psychosomatic illnesses or end up with nervous breakdowns.

*Look at what happens in a real rags-to-riches story (not including those who inherit their money or win a lottery): a refugee arrives with nothing. Well, actually you can't say that they have "nothing." They have motivation, energy, intelligence and they know how to achieve wealth. Instead of going after money itself, they <u>set in motion the **indirect processes**</u> that actually lead to wealth. They get an education. They network with others (interpersonal relations skills). They build relationships and connections that allow access to financial credit and to resources of power. If their goal is financial success only, they may limit their application of these principles to their wealth-building activities, missing out on other opportunities for different kinds of wealth.*

Any success that could be achieved <u>without</u> Extro • Dynamics in any of these areas — health, wealth or romance — would only be enhanced <u>with</u> it.

Of course, it is also crucial to remember that, because the goals of health, wealth and love are not strictly related to happiness, you can collect a lot of money and still be miserable; attain physical health and long life without being happy; or be romantically active without enjoying meaningful and satisfying relationships. Extro • Dynamics not only improves our chances for achieving these goals, but, more importantly, enables us to enjoy them after we get them.

Despite this clear acknowledgment of the separation between enjoying happiness and achieving success in these secondary goals, some will raise the question: "If we try to learn 'unselfish' lifestyle habits in order to obtain health, wealth, or love [for ourselves], is that <u>really</u> unselfish?"

While the enhancement of other (selfish) goals may motivate us to initiate an unselfish lifestyle, such motives may give us the push to get started, and allow us to set in motion the attitudes and behaviors that lead to truly unselfish feelings and actions. As long as that initial, underlying selfishness still dominates our motives, the goal of obtaining true happiness will remain elusive. When we have completed the transformation to true unselfishness, then everything else will fall into place.

Important Note: *This section relies heavily on the underlying concepts of Extro • Dynamics. At all times while reading this chapter, keep in mind the underlying approach: reaching away from self-preoccupation in a specific, active way. The specific suggestions in this chapter are designed to be implemented through the perspective of Extro • Dynamics.*

Okay, so you still want money, romance and a long and healthy life. Let's examine more closely how Extro • Dynamics can help you in each area:

7

Maximizing Financial Opportunity

Extro • Dynamics should not be confused with a "get-rich-quick" scheme. It is not a program for building wealth or making money, but the development of practical personal values that you can actually live by. It is important to reaffirm that when these values are put into daily practice from a genuinely unselfish perspective, they add to, not undermine, the prospects of financial security. Without proposing in-depth strategies for financial independence, we do wish to support our claim that Extro • Dynamics benefits financial security, and show some of the ways in which you can use these principles most effectively.

As with all situations in which this book promotes personal benefit, be careful to avoid the trap of reciprocal expectation, as noted above and in Chapter 6. As long as you seek to satisfy only selfish desires, true happiness will elude you. But if you set the course in motion and truly develop a *practical unselfishness* based on *all four steps,* opportunities for success can be maximized, along with the capacity for enjoying it after you get it!

To create great wealth from scratch (not from inheritance, gambling or merely processing paper transactions that transfer someone else's wealth to you), you must add value to the world. You must either create a great contribution, or else a small contribution that is widely distributed. For example, an investor may risk sizable capital assets on a single large project that provides jobs and creates goods and services, and enjoys financial wealth and

111

security commensurate with that contribution; or, as in the case of movie stars, sports figures, or other entertainers, it could be argued that the product they contribute (fun; entertainment) is trivial, but because it is transmitted through the mass media on such a scale as to affect many millions of people, their many small-scale contributions combine to create a total amount of wealth (enhanced quality of life) which is substantial.

On smaller scales of wealth production, workers who work harder and produce more improves whatever chances they have for advancement; merchants who make sure their customers are happy improve the outlook for success of their other business decisions; and employers who treat workers fairly, pay them well and create a pleasant work environment increase productivity, avoid the costs of employee turnover, and improve the quality of the products those workers produce.

On the contrary, efforts to gain wealth by living off the productivity of others are contrary to achieving long-term success. Any money is gained *despite* the failure to contribute, not because of it. It is like pointing to a 95-year-old who smokes and drinks as proof that such vices aren't really so bad for you, when the real question should be *how long would he have lived if he <u>didn't</u> do those things?* All other things being equal, people whose lifestyles radiate an active, practical compassion for others — "people skills" — will achieve greater wealth than if they did everything else exactly the same, but without good interpersonal relations skills. And when the whole model — *all four steps* — is implemented, potentials for success are greatly enhanced.

People who make their livings by cheating others may seem to receive financial benefit for a time, but in the long run may also risk business failure (including possibly going to jail if they are operating beyond the law). Just ask Michael Milken, Leona Helmsley, Ivan Boesky, Charles Keating, Ferdinand and Imelda Marcos, Jim and Tammy Bakker, along with other high-flyers from the "me-first" 1980's whose wealth was based on paper transfers of others' wealth, which ultimately came crashing down in flames of personal disaster. Even those who never get caught or pay for their "crimes" so overtly, if they are oriented only towards themselves, *will never achieve as much wealth as they would have if they had made a contribution to others.*

This phenomenon is now receiving considerable attention from the once-skeptical business community. Thomas Peters and Robert Waterman have analyzed various successful companies to demonstrate that "excellence" — the total contribution to customers and employees — is not merely an ethical consideration, but also a factor that contributes to financial success.

Robert Allen, the real estate wizard and motivational speaker who made millions with "Nothing Down" and by helping others replicate his success, repeatedly emphasizes in his books, tapes and lecturers that every deal must be "Win / Win" — financial success comes from identifying problems and helping people solve them.

Bob Basso, Ph.D., and his program of "Light Management," not only teaches businesses and employees workplace habits that are more ethical and enjoyable, but which allow everyone involved to make more money in the process. [Basso 1993 and 1986; Also Basso & Klosek]

The 1947 Christmas movie classic, "Miracle on 34th Street" is about a department store Santa Claus who defied the retail strategies of the times by sending customers to other stores if his didn't carry what they were looking for. He wasn't even thinking of earning more money, he just wanted what was best for the shoppers. Yet, in the movie, the goodwill generated by this gesture led to more sales than ever. Such an example may have seemed like Hollywood-style exaggeration in 1947; cute, but nothing that could occur in the real world. But in the 1990's, store clerks routinely give cheerful, helpful referrals to their competitors, and it is perceived as a practical promotional effort. Forty years ago this chapter would be much more difficult to write, because the idea of compassionate behavior as a serious business strategy would be sharply ridiculed. Today, while a few skeptics may remain, it is consistent with most economic strategies. And forty years in the future, this chapter won't even *need* to be written because it will seem so obvious!

The secret is out. In the words of Zig Ziglar, perhaps the premier motivational speaker of the 20th Century, "You can have everything in life you want if you will just help enough other people get what they want!" [Ziglar 1991, frontispiece.] A wide range of experts in wealth building and personal development, from Dale Carnegie and his *How to Win Friends and Influence People,* to Maxwell Maltz, M.D. and his *Psycho-Cybernetics,* to Norman Vincent Peale and his *Power of Positive Thinking,* to Napoleon Hill and his *Think and Grow Rich,* to Zig Ziglar and his motivational books, tapes and lectures, unanimously recognize, without any credible dissent, the importance of values once considered abstract and idealistic: positive mental attitude and effective "people skills" that not only promote a happy and ethical life, but financial success as well.

You can produce wealth either in conjunction with others in a company setting (as an employee, corporate officer or business owner), or through your own independent entrepreneurial investments (manufacturing products, providing housing through the real estate market or providing business or personal services to others). While the analysis of specific investments or business enterprises is beyond the scope of this book, the underlying principle that can guide you to financial security parallels the four steps in the Extro • Dynamics model:

1. Start from your own frame of reference — what are you good at? What do you *like* to do? Many who earn the *most* money just do the things they enjoy, in sports, entertainment, public affairs and other areas of business. How many times have you heard well-known personalities make the comment, "I can't believe they pay me to do this!" Identify business interests and activities that are compatible with the spirit of your own abilities, interests and personality. Marsha Sinetar develops this idea further in her book, *Do What You Love, The Money Will Follow.* If you don't believe you are capable of contributing to others, then your self-esteem is seriously handicapped, a "first-step" problem that must be remedied in order to achieve success with the other steps.

2. Move away from a focus centered around self-preoccupation, to a state "beyond self." What is the economic

environment you are operating in? Take a neutral, objective view of financial and economic realities.

3. Determine what other people need or want. Awareness of the feelings, values and needs of others is critical to the development of wealth strategies, since you must be able to provide that which will actually be of value to other people. Merge the value of what you want to contribute with the needs of others. How can you do what you want while benefiting others? Understand the desires and needs of clients, employers, co-workers and competitors *from their perspectives.* Identify ways to link your interests and abilities to the needs of others to produce real wealth.

4. Put your plan into *action! Do it now!* Stop being theoretical and *make a contribution.*

No matter what area(s) of investment you pursue, it is important to achieve financial wealth in the context of your over-all happiness and well being. Never lose sight of the contribution you are making to the economy and to the lives of those who benefit from the production of goods and services you produce.

If you work on an assembly line making auto parts, visualize the benefit you create for those who ultimately use your products — and keep that image in mind as you work for their benefit and for the benefit of the employer who provides that regular pay-check. The more valuable you make yourself as a contributor of value, the more easily you will find opportunities for advancement.

If you invest in real estate, visualize the ways in which human beings living in your properties, or those who buy houses you have fixed up for resale, benefit from reasonably priced quality residences, from someone who deals with them in a manner that is fair and reflects the depth of your commitment to creating real value.

Mark Neary is a very close friend of many years who has achieved great financial success in real estate investing and property ownership. I was with him once when someone asked him how he had been so successful. His answer: "I don't get greedy." He has numerous properties, and wants to maximize his investment. He sets initial rents below market rates. This results in a high number of applicants, so he can be selective in choosing the very best. This saves him money up front because he can get good, reliable tenants in a very short period of time, so units don't remain vacant long. If tenants prove to be as good as their applications suggested, he never raises their rent, so their initial bargain gets better and better through time and they stay in their units a long time, keeping overall vacancy levels to a minimum. Because they appreciate their great deals and want to stay on his good side, they don't bother him with petty or trivial concerns and they make sure to pay their rents on time. He avoids the cost of many minor repairs that tenants handle themselves, and the costs of evictions, unpaid rents, collections, etc., because he makes sure his tenants are so happy they would never do anything to jeopardize their great deal. It is truly a win-win deal. Tenants think (rightly) that they have the best deal ever. My friend has a small but steady profit margin with minimum hassle and expense.

Another close relative is in the real estate loan business. When she found out the high levels of points and charges some of her peers were charging, she was appalled. One agent asked her what she charged on a particular loan and he said, "How can you make any kind of profit on that kind of deal?" Her answer: "Because I sell a lot of them." Her critic said, "Yeah, but once I close the deal I'll never see these people again." She just thought to herself: "I bet you won't. But I plan to."

We all have business interactions that we look back on with regret, and others that we look back on as really great deals. The key to long-term success is making sure that the people who do business with you always look back on your deals as winners. Making people happy is just good business.

If you own your own business, consider the benefit that you contribute to your workers. You provide jobs and you create a pleasant and safe work environment. Think also of your customers, who create the demand for what you offer. If you always create true value and make sure that the needs of your customers are met to their real satisfaction, they will come back for more and recommend you to others. Many businesses give lip service to this concept, and perhaps even really believe it, but when it comes time to put in the extra time or effort for a higher quality of product or service (or pay others to), or it is time to allow a substantial price break, they lose sight of the long-term gains which become obscured by the immediacy of the up-front cost. And their shortsightedness will cost them in the long run.

What about selling (on commission)? Some might think of salesmanship as the very antithesis of Extro • Dynamics — a sharp salesperson engages an unsuspecting prospect in a competition: if the prospect wins, he gets to keep his money; if the seller wins, the prospect pays up and the seller gets his commission. While there are certainly some sellers who take that predatory, adversarial approach, think about the real skills of selling, and note how closely they parallel the four steps of Extro • Dynamics: 1) the seller must have self-esteem, self-confidence, appreciation of self value and motivation; 2) he must be able to break free of the restrictive limits of a self-centered perspective; 3) he must be able to view the entire sales process *through the prospect's perspective,* in order to answer questions or objections in a way that will elicit the desired response; 4) he must take direct action, whether in finding and meeting prospects or, in the sales process, to ask for a specific commitment and close the sale. In reality, everybody is a salesperson. Certainly, the raw mechanics of the sales process can be applied without enjoying the feelings and perspectives of Extro • Dynamics, but if they are incorporated as a complete package, the seller can enjoy not only more sales, but true happiness in determining the real needs of his clients and finding ways to help them get what they really want.

Whatever path you choose will be enhanced by following the Extro • Dynamics model. You must develop self-esteem and self-confidence and identify the activities that realistically match your interests and aptitudes; you must seek objectively the ways in which these areas address general needs; you must merge these two perspectives to develop *your* specific contribution as seen by others; and, you must take action to actually follow through with your plan. You are the only one who can do it. Others can provide ideas, assistance, feedback, suggestions, encouragement and help you to develop the resources and self-development skills necessary to use the Extro • Dynamics model. But *you* are the one who is ultimately responsible for your own financial destiny.

Some people doubt their ability to achieve financial success because they come from backgrounds of poverty or other disadvantage. Yet there are many examples of "rags-to-riches" success stories: those who achieved great wealth when they had every possible excuse for justifying failure.

The difference between the self-made wealthy and the poor is more than just the tangible accumulation of money. If you take all the money away from a rich person who is self-made, he will soon have it all back again. Recovery from such financial reversals happens all the time among the very wealthy. On the other hand, poor people who win lotteries often find that, in the long run, their lives are not changed all that much by simply adding money, while children who inherit the estates of the wealthy parents who failed to teach wealth-building skills to go along with the money, often squander such gifts.

What about someone born in the poverty of a remote, industrially-primitive "third-world" society? While the concepts presented in this chapter may be limited by the constraints of totalitarianism, feudalism or any system that restricts economic mobility by allowing one caste or class to dominate another, these principles can be used to *maximize any possible financial opportunities.*

When one considers Malala Yousafzai, a young girl born in the backwater mountains of the Swat Valley of Pakistan, in economic conditions far more humble than many Americans can possibly comprehend, and then being intimidated from education by bombings of schools and eventually the bullet of a gun, to see her rise to international leadership and prominence while still a teenager, one can appreciate that, yes, obstacles make things harder and will dissuade many, and barriers should be torn down, but with sufficient strength of soul, they can be overcome.

Others have risen from the destitution of being Holocaust survivors to achieve success in business and industry, or have risen from other conditions of poverty and privation to gain personal, social, community and economic success.

A lifestyle based on Extro • Dynamics leads to greater happiness and contentment, which builds morale, improves customer service, fosters good employee relationships and makes everyone more productive. Greater productivity promotes greater wealth.

It is no longer just a question of right and wrong or of being idealistic. You can "have your cake and eat it too." You can "have it all." You can be a good and moral person and still succeed financially. If you lose yourself in contributing to others, using the simple four-step model (including the adaptations for financial gain in this chapter) *you will improve your financial condition.* More importantly, your life will be rich and rewarding in the forms of wealth that are most truly rewarding.

Chapter 7 Summary

Strategies for achieving wealth are enhanced, not impaired, by living compassionately. Extro • Dynamics does not guarantee great wealth, but whatever level of financial success is attained will be greater with Extro • Dynamics than without it.

8

Success in
Romantic Love

Because success in romance is inherently based on interactions with another human being, perhaps among the three goals — health, wealth and romance — its link with Extro • Dynamics is perhaps most obvious.

As with happiness itself, love seems to fall capriciously into the lives of those who seem least concerned about it, while those who try hardest to find it seem to come up empty-handed and frustrated.

We want to share our lives with someone who is clever, funny, good-looking, kind, generous, intelligent and financially success-ful. But if we only think of our own wants, what makes us think we can ever get what we want? Why would a person who is clever, funny, cute and financially successful want to be involved with us if we are not clever, funny, good-looking, kind, generous, intelli-gent and financially successful ourselves? In the words attributed to French statesman Robert Schuman, "When I was a young man, I vowed never to marry until I found the ideal woman. Well, I found her, but unfortunately she was waiting for the perfect man." [Quoted in Ann Landers column dated 1-4-95.]

We must go beyond our own wants and desires, learning also to focus on what we can do to appeal to the needs or wants of someone else. We have to find the things that will make us attractive to the kind of person we seek. If we are not the kind of person that our ideal soul mate would cherish, we can use the Extro • Dynamics model to transform ourselves into that kind of person, as a caterpillar blossoms into a butterfly.

Because the Extro • Dynamics model is so flexible and simple, we can easily apply the steps to the various situations in our lives. Just as we adapted them to fit our financial goals in the previous chapter, they can also help transform us into cheerful, desirable, pleasant personalities to whom others are readily attracted:

1. Developing personal knowledge, skills and abilities gives us something we can contribute to others. Self-confidence, self-esteem and good feelings about ourselves let us actually achieve the full potential of what we can offer, and ensure that we won't let others treat us badly. By celebrating our own personal value and getting in touch with our own feelings, we have the capacity for sharing feelings with someone else.

2. By accepting and enjoying the equal value of another person, we become aware of their interests and needs, which is a prerequisite to making ourselves appeal to their desires and needs. We can combine our self-value and personal empowerment skills with the needs, feelings and equal value of another person — through a perspective of *their* viewpoint — and identify specific ways to bring our interests, needs and contributions into harmony with theirs.

3. Put your plan into *action! Do it **now!*** Stop being theoretical and *make a contribution.*

Once again, we must remember the problem of reciprocal expectation (see the section on positive relationships). While we do have legitimate needs to consider, the more we dwell on what *we* want from the relationship — the more we focus on self preoccupation — the less satisfying our relationships will be. However, when we lose ourselves in a *genuine* interest in the needs of those around us, and act accordingly, others will want us to be near us.

Authors Richard and Janet Reed describe the irresistibility of contributing cheerfully to others. By understanding their feelings and knowing how to become attractive to them, we can make ourselves irresistible. People will want us around because we make them feel comfortable. We can truly transform ourselves into a "Love Magnet." [Reed 1988]

Real understanding of the feelings and perspectives of our loved one includes overcoming feelings of possessiveness or jealousy. To any person who has mastered Extro • Dynamics, this will seem obvious; for any reader having difficulties in this area, it will be necessary to go back to the fundamentals. First, develop self-appreciation and self-value, and then work on the ability to lose yourself in a genuine interest in the personal value of your soul mate *from their point of view.* When you truly act in harmony with a cheerful contribution to another human being, you will automatically sense that equality is far more satisfying than superiority, sharing is better than dominating, and accepting the value of what the other person has to contribute benefits *both of you* more than holding them down so that you can feel superior. Genuine and unselfish feelings of Extro • Dynamics will not only result in allowing and encouraging the freedom and autonomy of your loved one, but even in *enjoying* their contribution more fully.

Let me relate an experience from my childhood, which does not involve a romantic situation, but helps illustrate this concept:

When I was young, I enjoyed a keen interest in birds, both wild and domesticated. I studied birds and enjoyed bird watching. I always had at least one pet bird, usually more, including parakeets, pigeons and assorted injured wild birds which neighbors would bring me to nurse back to health. I always freed the wild birds when they were able; domestic birds I did not, knowing that they would be unable to survive on their own and would quickly die in an environment they were not suited for. Almost everywhere I went I took a bird with me, even going to the supermarket or camping in the woods with a parakeet perched on my shoulder.

But in time, as school, work and other teenage activities competed for increasingly scarce time and attention, I no longer kept birds as day-to-day pets.

By the time I entered college, I found an alternative that required less daily attention. I noticed that there were always wild bluebirds (actually, California scrub jay, but it was blue and bird so I always called them "bluebirds") perched in the trees and sitting on the phone lines around my house. Each morning when I left, and each evening when I returned, I would throw a handful of peanuts on the back yard lawn, and the bluebirds would swoop down for the free feast as soon as I closed the sliding glass door. This allowed me to surround myself with birds without the daily chores of maintenance, care and feeding.

After some time, I started throwing the peanuts onto the lawn, but I stood in the sliding glass doorway without closing it. After a brief hesitation, the birds would come down and take the peanuts. After several weeks of this, I threw out the peanuts, but closed the sliding glass door while I remained out on the lawn with the birds. Little by little I moved closer and closer to where the birds picked up their free treasures, until I was very near to them.

Eventually, I sat on the ground and held the peanuts in my hand, keeping my hand very near the ground so they could snatch the peanuts without actually entering my hand. This caused the birds great hesitation, but eventually one of them tried it and was rewarded with his usual treat without any real danger. I gradually raised my hand higher and higher until the birds had to alight on my hand in order to take their treasures.

Not all of the birds were willing to do so. Only about three individual birds would take the peanuts from my outstretched hand. Two of them would fly quickly past, grab a peanut as fast as possible, and fly away. One little female, however, would sit on my hand comfortably, taking as long as necessary to pick up several peanuts. She would sit in the tree or on the phone lines and, when she saw me coming, would swoop down and alight gently on my open hand. She would even sit on my hand and take peanuts that I placed inside my mouth. (Imagine, in terms of our relative sizes, the trust she had to feel in order to put her tiny body inside the mouth of a monster-sized being like me, just to get a peanut.) I treasured his special friendship for about six years.

Since childhood, I had enjoyed "owning" many birds. But none was as special as this little bluebird, because I knew that she was not *forced* to come to me because I had bought her from a breeder or rescued her from injury. I attracted her so that she came to me by her own free choice. There was no possessiveness or ownership.

And I never had a better "pet" (until replicating the process and the result later as an adult).

The same is true in all relationships. In romance, it is not necessary to hold on to loved ones through possessiveness, coercion or by trying to hold them down. When we respect the personal dignity and integrity of those whose lives we share, and attract them to us by the contribution we offer them, then they come freely and by choice. We may wish someone to find us attractive or lovable, and suffer disappointment when they don't. But we cannot change their feelings by coercion or force. Any possibility of changing their feelings would be the result of following the four-step model: understanding *their* feelings and *taking action* to make them feel comfortable and happy by *attraction* rather than *coercion*. And if there is no hope of such an attraction, the re-direction of our preoccupations away from self will enable us to accept that reality more graciously. There is no greater enjoyment of truly feeling loved than to know that love is given willingly and eagerly, not because it is coerced or forced. In the words of psychiatrist M. Scott Peck, describing real and sincere love, "Two people love each other only when they are quite capable of living without each other but *choose* to live with each other." [Peck p. 98]

It is not necessary to dominate or control. Relationships do not need a "leader" or "follower." A man whose insecurity (weak first step) makes him feel a need to dominate women may simultaneously satisfy the universal human need for social companionship by going "out with the boys," where friendship is enjoyed and activities planned without "leaders" or "followers." Or an insecure woman may suffer from feelings of jealousy, possessiveness or an unwarranted lack of trust and attempt to control the activities and associations of her loved one but may, at the same time, enjoy other friendships without these destructive symptoms of self-obsession.

Those who seek control or domination over their loved ones — like those who pursue happiness directly, like an object — are not happy people. They are tense and uptight. Possessive or controlling actions, as with other compulsive behaviors, are not manifestations of the desire for happiness, but attempts to reduce insecurity and anxiety. Mariah Burton Nelson, in her book *The Stronger Women Get, The More Men Love Football*, writes that insecure men seek protection from the perceived threat of strong women by retreating behind sports and "macho" symbolic toughness. (See also Chapter 13, "Competitiveness.")

There are some who seek to dominate or control or sexually harass others, but wish they could stop doing so. It's not so easy to just stop, because their obsessive, compulsive possessiveness is like an addiction. The only way to break free of that self-oriented, jealous urge is to change the underlying self-directedness that causes it. In each case the cure involves going through *all four* of the steps which lead away from the self-preoccupation so central to compulsive habits: Adequate self worth, breaking free from a purely self-centered perspective, appreciation of the equal value and dignity of another person and bringing them together in a sharing through the other person's viewpoint, and action to reflect and express those feelings and perspectives. Friendship, equal sharing and pleasant camaraderie in romantic relationships are not obligations we "have to" do just because it's "right" (though it *is* right) but also because *it makes the relationship better!* Humans are not birds, but as with my little wild bluebird, the greatest pleasure in relationships comes when relationships are free and spontaneous, by attraction rather than coercion.

Another important part of romance involves sexuality. When sexuality is pursued directly, as a self-contained goal of pleasure for its own sake, some pleasure may be enjoyed. But a relationship based primarily on sexual pleasure will eventually become stale and boring as the novelty wears off and the "spice" loses its alluring and enticing spontaneity. In fact, when sexual pleasure is removed far enough from a sharing of real closeness with another person, it can degenerate into a bodily function not much more satisfying than scratching an itch or going to the bathroom. As actor Woody Harrelson said to Greg Laurie, "No matter how many beautiful women I was with, it was never enough." [Rivenburg, p. E2]. As we have reiterated many times, the direct pursuit of pleasure as selfishness never leads to real fulfillment.

On the other hand, when the spice is shared and nurtured in mutual selflessness, as an ongoing process of sharing common interests, activities and values, the relationship not only avoids becoming stale, but it becomes even more exciting. Like other *processes of consciousness,* passion becomes more intense when it is an *ongoing process* of energy rather than an object of direct physical pursuit. It is really pathetic to see someone consumed with self-preoccupation in the pursuit of sexual pleasure, trying one new technique or device or person after another, always looking for another "kick," yet never really achieving a joyful and sensual satisfaction. (Even if they achieve the specific goal of a romance or marriage or whatever, as long as it is a "tangible" static goal, it will settle into a dull and unsatisfying rut after the milestone has been passed.) The solution is so simple: let go! Use Extro • Dynamics to reach away from selfishness in creating an active, spontaneous pleasure for the one you share your life with.

Explore the magic fully! Let it be a function of relationship — in whatever form is right for you — reaching away from purely self-directed attention, to an intense sharing of the pleasure you create for another person to be shared completely. When sexuality and romance are enhanced in this way, they grow and deepen, remaining exciting and stimulating for many years — even into very advanced age.

Chapter 8 Summary
Love and romance are the essence of relationship. Extro • Dynamics, which enriches all forms of relationship, can add new dimensions of feeling, excitement and active sharing when either or both partners reaches beyond self to deeper and more satisfying levels.

9

A Long and Healthy Life

We regard with reverent awe the reputed longevity of the Tibetan Buddhist monks, as well as that of others in isolated communities where unusually lengthy life spans are reported. The Dalai Lama writes about the curiosity of Westerners regarding this seemingly supernatural longevity, and minimizes the influence of occult factors [Dalai Lama, 1990]. Tibetan Buddhists teach a philosophy of meditation, relaxation and compassion and live long to 100 or more in excellent health.

Respected medical experts suggest that the human body should not "wear out" from true old age for about 120 years [Walford 1986 & 1983]. When humans follow lifestyles conducive to long and healthy lives, in accordance with natural law, they will live a long time. No "magic" is involved.

The related issues of health, longevity and physical well-being have a uniquely circular relation to Extro • Dynamics. Physical well-being is, in conjunction with other aspects of the first step, *causal to* the remaining steps; it is also, along with other factors, *caused by* completion of all the steps.

The first step of Extro • Dynamics is to look inward to self value and take care of basic needs, including physical well-being. Good physical health prevents pain and illness which force attention toward self-preoccupation in unpleasant ways. Additionally, good health affords the strength and energy to be able to reach away from the self and into the surrounding environment to operate on it in ways that are active and stimulating.

There is a wide and confusing assortment of books, tapes and self-development programs that claim to improve health or longevity or both. Which are worthwhile? Which are scams? As with all aspects of personal development, there is never just a single answer. And while this chapter provides excellent information you can use in your daily lifestyle routine, it is also strongly recommended that you consult a wide range of competent sources for additional information about topics of interest to you.

While there may be a few incompetent (or even malicious) quacks running around, many of the programs offer valid approaches that differ only because each represents only one part of the overall picture. To achieve the best results in terms of both quantity of life (longevity) and quality of life (health), it is best to develop well-balanced health habits that integrate the most successful elements of various reputable approaches, which can be divided into three categories: **Exercise, Diet** and a cheerful, positive mental outlook, or **Attitude**. When combined, these can lead to the greatest potential for physical well-being.

These three elements reinforce each other and work together. None can provide maximum benefit without the others. As described by noted cardiologist Dr. Dean Ornish, Just as a fire needs a combination of air, heat and fuel to burn, your physical well-being needs all three components, integrated into an ongoing lifestyle pattern that fits your personality and interests in a way that you can enjoy and keep up with. [Ornish, 1998]

Vigorous exercise stimulates a healthy appetite and regulates metabolic processes so that food can be used for energy rather than stored as fat. A naturally healthy diet lets you feel light and energetic, ready for physical activity. Diet and exercise together minimize susceptibility to illness and fatigue, and release natural chemicals called endorphins that generate pleasant feelings of well being and contentment. A positive, cheerful attitude provides additional health benefits and also enhances the motivation and optimism to initiate and stick with your new diet and exercise plan. [Cooper 1982 and Ornish 1990]

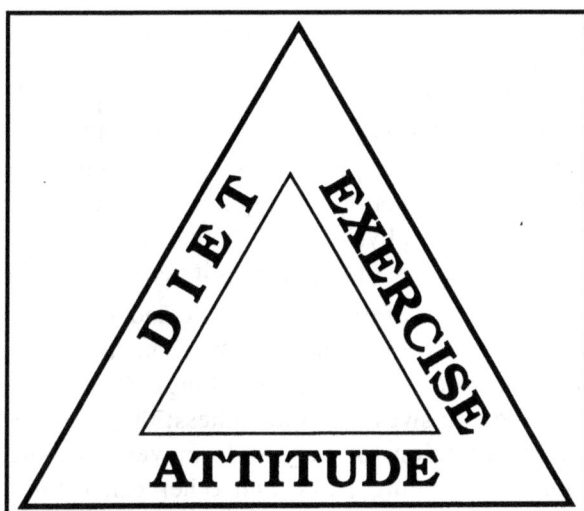

Physical well-being cannot be maximized until all the pieces are integrated into a complete, balanced whole.

In addressing each of these components, make sure you maintain the selfless perspective of Extro • Dynamics. Keep it fun — a *process* of *activity*. Don't fight with it — find the ways to fit each element into your lifestyle and preferences. If you have survived with your bad habits a long time, it will be difficult to make a sudden and drastic change. You took a long time to wear down your body, take the time to gradually ease into new long-range routines that you can really stick with. Find exercise routines that are fun. Find healthy and nutritious foods that you enjoy eating. And use Extro • Dynamics to keep your mental attitude positive, cheerful and upbeat.

As with success in financial security or romance, the link between Extro • Dynamics and health is indirect. Some who "pump iron" or eat healthy diets are not necessarily compassionate. But there are also many surprising links between health and the steps of Extro • Dynamics, as we will show in this chapter. If you follow the simple four-step model and the specific suggestions in this chapter, you will have a longer and healthier life than if you don't. And, even when setbacks occur, you can resist them better and recover from them faster.

Exercise. The emergence of human life occurred in an environ-ment that imposed strenuous demands for physical exertion in order to survive. Our bodies developed and grew in response to the stimulation of physical activity. Although our high-tech civilization has preempted many of the survival aspects that underlie our need for vigorous and regular exercise, our bodies will not provide maximum physical well being unless we provide the stimulation and challenge of the activity it needs.

There are two kinds of exercise: aerobic and anaerobic. Aerobic exercises (from the word coined by Dr. Kenneth H. Cooper) are those that stimulate the heart and lungs (the cardiovascular system), leaving you sweaty and breathless; they generally consist of many rapid repetitions of easy-to-do movements, such as running, swimming, jumping jacks, and other calisthenics [Cooper 1968]. Anaerobic exercises are those that develop strength in specific muscles with a few strenuous repetitions, such as doing push-ups or pull-ups to strengthen the arms, or sit-ups to strengthen the tummy. Anaerobic exercises are important so that you can enjoy the strength necessary for certain sports or activities that you may wish to participate in, but aerobic exercises are the ones which are truly vital for longevity and over-all physical well-being. The heart and lungs provide crucial ongoing support, not only to the muscles, but to every cell in the body. A strong cardiovascular system not only prevents heart disease, stroke and other illnesses, but also just makes you feel better: more energetic, more alert, more active, and more eager to reach into the surrounding environment and enjoy life to the fullest — not just as a spectator, but as a participant!

To implement an integrated, balanced program of aerobic and anaerobic exercises that match your lifestyle and personality, follow certain precautions:

1. If you have any known or suspected preexisting medical conditions, consult your physician or medical practitioner first. While your exercise program should offer benefit to any illness or condition, you want to make sure that your activity does not conflict with other aspects of treatment, and that you don't move too quickly (or too slowly!) in pacing the development of your new exercise regimen.

2. Keep it fun! Do you like to swim? Play tennis? Golf? Throw a Frisbee? Some enjoy the quiet solitude of running alone, letting their minds wander or listening to the radio, or enjoying light conversation while running with a friend, while others find running tedious and boring. If you enjoy it, then do it. If it turns you off, find something you *do* like, and *do it!*

3. Develop your program gradually. My own aerobic exercise has consisted, at its peak, of doing 24 straight minutes of jumping jacks while listening to the news on the radio, at a pace of more than one per second, following a ten-minute of stretching warm-up, which I maintained for a number of years. But I didn't just go out one day and start doing 1,500 jumping jacks. I started with two minutes for the first two weeks. That seemed pretty easy. Then I added another minute for the next two weeks. Every other week I added another minute. It took me a year to get up to 20 minutes, but little by little it wasn't difficult. And, there was no hurry. It's a long-term commitment, not a quick fix. Two minutes was easy — not just in doing the exercise but also in finding (or making) the time for it. Maybe you'll start with one minute. Or thirty seconds. Or maybe you won't do jumping jacks at all because you're swimming, or playing tennis or racquetball.

4. Stick with a regular program. Set aside a regular time of the day for your exercise. You may prefer to do yours after work, when you're tired and need a pick-up. Whatever time is best for your lifestyle and preferences, stick with it. If your exercise is part of a recreational activity, make sure you include enough huffing and puffing and that, even though it is fun, you follow through with the amount of time you reserved for your physical well-being.

When you find the right *process of activity* for you, keep it fun, so your thoughts can drift away from self absorption, and make it gradually but uncompromisingly a part of your daily habits. Good mental attitude makes it easier to stick with your exercise program, and a good exercise program enhances good mental attitude!

Diet. How do our eating habits relate to living compassionately? There are two important ways: 1) reversal of diet-related compulsions and obsessions; and, 2) compassionate eating habits that are more natural and healthful to humans.

Reversing compulsions. When changing our eating habits to reflect a more healthful diet, we often become obsessed with thoughts of the foods that we miss from our old habits. This undermines our efforts and tempts us back towards our old ways. Extro • Dynamics helps to reverse these obsessions with the self-directed desires of old food memories, and help us focus instead on processes of action and outward direction that reduce or eliminate old cravings. This helps us to stick with the diet plans that we know will make us look better, feel better and live longer.

Extro • Dynamics can play an important role not only in motivating you to seek a healthy diet, based on the first step, or to provide the rationale for a compassion-based diet, but also makes it easier to stick with the new routine by overcoming the self-defeating cravings that cause most diets to fail.

When I decided to seek a healthier diet, I was concerned about all of the favorite foods that I would have to give up. But Extro • Dynamics helped me think positively instead of negatively. I wrote out a list of all the healthy things I really like and *can* eat and enjoy, and was surprised at how many of my favorite foods would still be available! So any time I start to feel limited, I pull out my list and start drooling over something that had momentarily slipped my mind. In time, your tastes and preferences change, returning to those that are more natural for humans, and the thought of eating the same food you used to enjoy becomes revolting instead of something you miss.

Eating naturally and *compassionately*: A diet that does not depend on killing other highly sentient creatures[1] is healthier, and more closely resembles the natural diet of our species.

The American diet, heavy with sweets, fats, additives and chemicals, bears little resemblance to that which sustained either our earliest human ancestors or the primate members of the animal kingdom such as gorillas, orangutans, gibbons and chimpanzees which are most biologically similar to ourselves.

So what? We like our red meat, pizza, chocolates and fast foods. A meat- and fat-based diet has served generations of Americans. "If it ain't broke, don't fix it." But why is it that, when biologists say we should be capable of living to ages of 100 and up, that so many of us die in our 50's, 60's and 70's and call it "old age." It's broke.

To "fix it" we must make sure that we ingest all needed nutrients, while avoiding the toxins and unhealthy substances that reduce physical vigor and shorten our life spans. While it may be trite to say so, this means enjoying a *balanced* diet. But what does "balance" mean? We hear the term often, but it is not defined often enough.

A tale of three heart doctors: Dr. Dean Ornish [Ornish, 1990] is a cardiologist who developed an extremely low-fat diet that concentrated on fruits, grains and vegetables from plant sources. In contrast, another cardiologist, Dr. Robert C. Atkins [Atkins, 1972] offered a heart-healthy plan that was almost the diametric opposite: high in fats and proteins, but extremely low in carbohydrates. A 2005 study reported in the 2005 *Journal of the American Medical Association* [Dansinger, et al, p. 43-53] compared the two diets head-to-head in a controlled experiment (along with Weight Watchers and Zone diets), and found both to be about equally

---

[1]"Sentient creatures" refers to animals with consciousness of the same type (though perhaps in different quantity) as ours. It would not refer to animals so low on the evolutionary scale as to be without real sentient consciousness, and would be proportionate to the degree of sentience, though it is beyond the scope of this work to explore such quantification with any degree of detail. This criterion would also exclude plant life forms, although the eating of most fruits, grains and vegetables does not kill the plant, but rather helps the plant spread its seeds and roots.

effective when strictly adhered to. In 2003, a third cardiologist, Dr. Arthur Agatston of Florida, claiming respect and friendship with both Atkins and Ornish, introduced a balanced, hybridized alternative, which he called the "South Beach Diet" [Agatston, 2003]. Instead of emphasizing cutting back just on carbohydrates (like Atkins) or just on fats (like Ornish) — all of the diet plans encourage proteins — he went to a deeper level of discernment: he noted that there are good fats (unsaturated fats, especially mono-unsaturated, Omega-3 fatty acids, etc.) and bad fats (saturated fats, LDL cholesterol). There are also good carbohydrates (fiber, complex whole grains) and bad carbohydrates (simple sugars and starches).

Agatston's approach, which seems to *balance* the best of the seemingly irreconcilable approaches of both Ornish and Atkins, is to encourage good nutrients (good carbs, good fats and proteins) and discourage bad nutrients (bad carbs and bad fats). In this way he comes up with a greater degree of balance. Unfortunately, his plan was made public too late to be included in the *JAMA* study.

Our bodies did not develop or evolve for diets that require the killing of other highly sentient beings. As with our closest biological relatives, our bodies originally developed in an environment rich in fruit, grain, nut and vegetable food resources, and evolved to thrive on those resources that were abundant in the primeval surroundings from which our species emerged. These are the foods that are high in fiber and complex carbohydrates, and low in bad forms of fat and other harmful substances. Our dental structures, digestive systems and other physiological traits are similar to those animals that eat produce, and are very different from meat-eating species. This suggests that such foods are the ones that are natural for our bodies and which should be central to our dietary habits. [Robbins 1987; Ornish 1990 and 1982; Diamond 1985]

As reported extensively by science writer Elaine Morgan, evidence also suggests a possibility that, in the course of our evolutionary differentiation from earlier hominoids, as the earliest human ancestors descended from trees and into savannahs, that they also likely found refuge near protective bodies of water, where they were able to find new food sources such as fish and other kinds of seafood, and perhaps escape predators by retreating into water. In fact, even today more than 90% of humans worldwide live within 100 miles of an ocean shoreline. Humans enjoy a great affinity for water and aquatic recreation which is extremely rare among other primates and show signs of physical adaptation such as hairlessness, vocal and auditory modes of communication similar to marine mammals and standing erect (keeping head, which retains hair, out of the water) as well as frontal sexual engagement [Morgan, 1990, 1972]. As a result, unlike other anthropoids, we evolved with a strong biological affinity for the kinds of nutrients in such aquatic food sources. While meat from mammalian sources such as cows (beef) or pigs (pork, ham, sausage) contains toxic saturated fats, fish and seafood sources provide beneficial types of monounsaturated fats and helpful Omega-3 fatty acids. Additionally, aquatic food sources are farther removed from sentient consciousness.

Still, in terms of eating compassionately, many do not believe that taking the life of *any* vertebrate is appropriate, no matter how minimally-developed their frontal lobes of consciousness might be. And, in fact, a strong case can be made for a vegetarian lifestyle that does not require the killing of any vertebrate (though allows for such foods as milk and eggs that can be amassed without taking the life of the animal) or even completely eschewing all animal products, as the vegans. This view, also, can be supported by appeals to basic human nature.

Imagine you're walking through a beautiful forest and stumble across the day-old carcass of a cow. What's your reaction? Are you hungry? Or does this sound gross? A real carnivore, like a wolf or leopard, would be licking his chops — he likes to eat his meat raw, including the raw guts, too [Lilly & Montero, adapted from the foreword by William Belote].

If you think it's natural for humans to eat meat, put a three-year-old toddler in a crib with an apple and a live chicken and watch which one he eats and which one he plays with. If you give the same apple and chicken to a young cat of equivalent maturity, it will play with the apple and eagerly kill and eat the chicken, all by itself!

You protest, "Whaddayamean a meat-based diet isn't natural? Meat is central to the diet in almost every known civilization on earth!" That is true. But all human peoples trace their origins to the early humans that developed in North Africa. At a time when the feeding and breeding grounds of that region were changing from a lush tropical paradise into a harsh, scorching desert, survival of our species demanded that we either retreat deeper into the continent, as some species did, or diversify our diets. Perhaps the first regular use of meat was revolting and unpleasant. But it occurred around the same time as another milestone in human development: control of fire. Our ancestors put the two together so they could survive. By cooking the meat and adding spices and sauces and seasonings they could disguise its revolting, unnatural flavor and learn to like it. After eating it enough, people not only learned to like it, but they got addicted to it. Eating meat kept our ancestors alive long enough to have offspring and pass along their genes, but they paid a high price for it in shortened lifespan and loss of physical strength compared with other primates who are almost exclusively vegetarian. Even today, we eat fruits, vegetables, grains and nuts in a fairly natural condition, but we still disguise our meat so it has very little resemblance to the natural carcass that a true carnivore would savor.

Today we are no longer at the brink of survival. We no longer need meat. Like many animals, such as elephants, hippopotami and the livestock that we use for food, our bodies can produce plenty of bulk, strength and energy entirely from plant sources. Even the largest of man's closest relatives, gorillas and orangutans, have plenty of body size, and its all strength, on a purely vegetarian diet.

Does this mean that we should never eat anything except "rabbit food"? My own choice is a diet that does not include any meat from mammals. That's *my* decision. If health factors are your primary concern, occasional servings of meats, fats, or sweets, limited to special occasions only, should not cause permanent damage. A person can enjoy good health and still practice Extro • Dynamics without becoming a vegetarian. However, consistent with the way compassion affects other areas of life, I consider it to be more than mere coincidence that *eating compassionately* is also the healthiest alternative.

Of course, meat is not the only harmful substance. Alcohol, tobacco and any drugs not related to medical treatment are poisons that shorten life span, weaken the body and reduce energy, vitality and an overall feeling of physical well-being, while opening the body up as a target for diseases of all types. With your newfound optimism and positive attitude about yourself and self worth, you will no longer have any wish to tolerate purely self-destructive habits. And when Extro • Dynamics has led you to a life of truly satisfying relationships that are happy, joyous and free, you will no longer need to pursue the desperate attempts to get "kicks" to escape from a dreary and unfulfilled existence.

As with your exercise program, develop a dietary plan that fits *your* tastes, *your* lifestyle and *your* needs. Do you need to lose weight? Gain weight? What foods do you like? If you plan eating habits based on things you don't really want to eat but feel you have to, your whole strategy becomes a battle of willpower. Don't make it hard on yourself! The key should be *attraction* rather than *obligation*. If you are under medical treatment of any kind, be sure to coordinate your selections with your medical practitioner. This is *your* diet — make sure it's one *you* can thrive on!

Additionally, I like to remember that science has now discovered many of the chemical properties of vitamins, nutrients and trace elements that can prolong life and add vitality and energy. I do take a multivitamin every day, as well as supplements that have been selected in consultation with my healthcare providers to match *my* specific and unique needs. Depending on weight, metabolism, energy level, and other unique genetic factors, each person's needs in this regard will vary. I encourage everyone to do the research based on their needs, consult with doctors and other healthcare experts, and find a total program of mental health, exercise, and diet, with appropriate vitamins, minerals and other supplements, designed for their needs.

As in your exercise program, don't make sudden and drastic changes that you won't be able to stick with. You're looking at a lifetime plan, not an overnight fad. You took many years to get addicted to self-destructive habits, so *gradually* phase out the old ones and phase in the new ones on a timetable that is right for you. Get out a calendar and write down a schedule on which harmful items will be reduced, and on which new favorites will be increased. Be specific. You may find it beneficial to eliminate one item at a time. The only exceptions are for highly addictive toxins such as alcohol, tobacco and hard drugs — in such cases, going "cold turkey" is usually more effective, particularly in conjunction with support from a self-help group. But for other harmful substances, such as fats, sweets and other chemical additives, a gradual change reduces the shock to the system and makes it easier for you to achieve success comfortably.

Again, as in your exercise program (note how consistently these principles reinforce each other), follow through with *all* the steps to set in motion a process that integrates your new behavior into a daily lifestyle pattern. Don't let your new eating habits become an obsession. Use Extro • Dynamics to reach away from self-preoccupation. Dwell on the positive aspects of what you *can* enjoy, and visualize all the fun things your newfound health will allow you to do, and you will avoid becoming trapped in dietary obsessions.

Attitude. Just as physical well being is a critical part of the first step, so it is also true that the cheerful selflessness that results from completing the model and integrating them into your day-to-day habits contributes to the positive mental attitude which is a basic component for physical well-being.

Just as a positive mental attitude and self-worth contribute to financial wealth and romantic success, the link between the reduction of psychological stress factors and an increase in optimistic, positive mental attitudes for the enhancement of good health is equally well-established, whether seen as "miraculous" recoveries, preventing disease from occurring in the first place, or just living a long and vital life. [Ornstein & Sobel 1989; Ornish 1982; Restak 1984, pp. 176-181.]

The Extro • Dynamics lifestyle contributes to a sense of contentment, happiness and well-being, which improves health; and good health promotes the good feelings and positive, cheerful outlook that facilitates the practice of Extro • Dynamics, in a feedback loop that could be called the opposite of a "vicious circle" — more like a "delicious circle."

And as was noted in the chapter on implementing a regular practice of the steps, when those times arise that you just "don't feel like it," and the feedback loop turns more negative and counterproductive, act out the part — "fake it 'til you make it" — and by acting in a manner that exudes optimism and sunny cheerfulness, you can slide back into that comfortable feeling of the Extro • Dynamics lifestyle.

Other aspects of developing a positive mental outlook include reducing stress. Make sure you are organizing your life to balance work, family, social community and recreational activities in a way that allows for adequate sleep (possibly reinforced by occasional daytime naps or siestas for interim refreshment and tension reduction) and, if necessary, get professional advice and counsel in making this work so as not to turn negative and focus attention back towards self-obsession.

In the early 1970's, studies showed that stressfully compulsive, nervous behavior driven by impatient, self-directed anxieties (called "Type A" behavior) resulted in a far higher incidence of heart attack than occurred in non-Type A behavior [Friedman & Rosenmann 1974]. More recent studies at the Duke University Behavioral Research Center showed that this was especially true when such self-motivated anxieties are specifically driven by anger and hostility, which they called "Type H" for hostile [Williams & Williams, 1996] .

The human spirit or consciousness is the controlling force that directs its physical tool, the body. Integrating Extro • Dynamics into everyday habits addresses the very source of happiness and positive psychic energy by re-directing attention from self towards positive, cheerful and stress-free interactions. While Extro • Dynamics is central to all aspects of getting what you want, nowhere is that more evident than this area of positive mental attitude.

And so we come full circle: mental and spiritual efficacy, as part of the first step, not only have a causal influence in enhancing other steps, but successfully implementing all the steps leads back to physical well-being, in an ongoing cycle. Once we set the process in motion it develops a life of its own. Our cheerful lifestyle becomes easy and automatic, and we no longer have to monitor it consciously. In conjunction with proper diet and enjoyable exercise activities, the Extro • Dynamics model will allow you to achieve whatever potential you were born with for good health and maximum life span.

Chapter 9 Summary

Lifestyles that are consistent with compassion and reaching away from self into all the activities and stimulation of the surrounding environment, lead not only to lives that are longer and healthier, but also rich in happiness and the satisfaction of true self-fulfillment. Such lifestyles integrate a balance of *good diet, good exercise* and *good attitude* through Extro • Dynamics.

Contemporary Issues

The great issues of our time are inter-connected. As we look around the world we see many problems competing for our attention and resources: civil rights, poverty, homelessness, crime, education, and the economy.

Compassion in community affairs, as in our personal lives, is not only right, but also most effective in providing long-range solutions to problems. It is important to note, however, that while public policy must be consistent with compassionate values, our tradition of personal freedom does not allow us to try to compel compassionate feelings or legislate personal moral beliefs. It is crucial, however, that we encourage compassion as a community value, and that we absolutely reject behavior that allows people to hurt each other.

What kind of policies might be developed by a community operating on the ideals of **practical** *compassion as represented in Extro • Dynamics? There is no single answer. Honest seekers of truth, from purely unselfish motives, may evaluate conditions differently and offer differing alternatives as solutions. The ideas that I have recommended in this section represent one viewpoint, based largely on my experience in dealing with community issues and problems. Differing opinions might just as well be offered, if the justifications are rooted in Extro • Dynamics.*

My proposals for a **practical** *compassion-based public policy are aimed, not only at the symptoms of problems, but at the underlying causes of those ills. This is not to say that symptoms should not be treated, but we must also cure the disease itself. Otherwise, we spend all our public resources putting ambulances at the bottom of the cliff instead of a fence at the top.*

10

Equality & Dignity

Much of my community experience has involved work with those from different cultural, ethnic, racial and national backgrounds, or artificial barriers erected based on gender or sexual orientation. In our modern world, sadly, such differences are often the basis for discrimination, tension and intercultural friction. A compassion-based perspective, through Extro • Dynamics, reveals these differences for the trivial superficiality they really represent, and causes any discrimination or frictions to quickly evaporate.

Many people who travel abroad or who meet people who represent different cultural perspectives do not really see the world from the very different viewpoints of those they encounter. Often such encounters are brief or superficial, and the richness of another person's culture is easily overlooked.

Yet if we open ourselves up to the perspectives of others and truly share an active involvement with them using the Extro • Dynamics model, we can broaden our cultural experiences to include new insights and a broadening of our global perspectives.

In sharing the perspectives of those from differing backgrounds, it would be simplistic to simply dismiss the truly great differences that separate populations whose historical, religious and cultural outlooks may be completely foreign to us. However, as we get to know the unique personalities of the individuals from those populations, we also discover that the cultural differences — while very real — are also superficial. "Culture" is a mask through which group perceptions are filtered and understood, and by which individuals within groups are able to communicate shared experiences. But the individual personality of a specific person is separate from the group experience. And within each culture group there are wide-ranging differences in individual personalities.

Whether in America or Africa or Europe or Asia of the 1990's, or in any other place in any other historical time period, the daily habits and customs of people, as well as differences in science, knowledge, technology and social institutions, may be very different. But in the specific temperaments of individuals, there are common threads that are strikingly similar. In each culture, in every place and time throughout the world and its history, some people are boisterous and aggressive, while others are shy and timid; some people are cruel and malicious, while others are kind, gentle and benevolent; some people are sociable and gregarious, while others enjoy quiet privacy; some people are intellectual and educated, while others are not; some people work with their hands, while others are oriented to issues and ideas; some people are spontaneous and original, while others are systematic and carefully organized. In every culture, no matter how different the superficial mask, there is a generous mix of each personality type.

In meeting and sharing interactions with those from different cultural backgrounds, once we break through the surface stereotypes and get to know the specific personalities of individuals, through *their* perspectives, two very strong impressions emerge: how different the cultural perspectives and behavioral expectations really are, yet how similar the underlying value and personalities of specific individuals are.

While day-to-day habits and cultural traditions may be different, there is more similarity and compatibility between a reserved, intellectual personality type from present-day America and his counterpart from an ancient African civilization than between two individuals from the same place and time but with incompatible personalities.

While there may be some room for debate as to how much learned cultural values and social traditions influence individual personality development, any notion that differences in skin color, race or other physical attributes (apart from culture), can influence personality is entirely absurd. Within each "racial" subgroup, there are differences in the coloration of eyes and hair as well as other physical differences. While differences in the coloration of skin may be more obvious or striking than differences in hair or eyes, it is no more important, nor of any greater personal significance in its effect on individual personality.

Modern scientists in the fields of biology and anthropology discount that any valid, measurable, empirical essence of racial distinction even exists. The common perceptions of racial characteristics are randomly-ascribed superficial physical attributes that do not support differentiation in classification by "race." Even the use of these superficial and largely irrelevant features cannot be reliably quantified or measured, as evidenced by the difficulties in classifying borderline cases in countries where legal discrimination required it. In other words, the existence of "race" is a tragic cultural myth. [Hotz, p. A1; Begley, pp. 67-69]

Tensions between "racial" or ethnic groups exist because people of one culture-group see those from different backgrounds as members of *groups* rather than as *individuals,* based on flawed assumptions and faulty observations.

Such a tendency is one of the more immature aberrations of human behavior. An event that occurred when I worked as a day-camp counselor while attending college, clearly shows how easy it is for people to classify others into groups on a purely superficial basis, and how childish it is.

While driving a group of children in a small minivan on the way to an activity, four children were sitting together in the middle seat. All of a sudden one little boy made an observation: three of them were wearing blue tennis shoes. One was wearing red tennis shoes. Once that simple and unimportant difference was observed, they began to separate themselves from the child who was "different" building up a very silly basis for differentiation and isolation, until the ridiculousness of it all was brought to their attention. It is easy for us to see the insanity of judging people by the color of their shoes, because that is not *our* choice in prejudices. But judging people by the color of their skin or hair or eyes is just as childish.

The same point was made in a cartoon from the strip "For Better or for Worse," by Lynn Johnston (9-19-96):

FOR BETTER OR FOR WORSE *by LYNN JOHNSTON*

The model presented in this book provides the solution to problems of racial, cultural and ethnic tensions. Once you begin to make it a regular part of your ongoing interactions, sharing and enjoying the individual value of each person you meet, stereotypes are quickly stripped away and individual personal value emerges. It becomes quickly obvious that the others around us, no matter what color their skin, eyes or hair, or what their religious or ethnic background is, or whether they are male or female, all have feelings and values and needs and drives. Each person is unique and special, and their unique personal value is not impaired or affected by superficial differences. When human beings learn to look beyond the surface differences, into the minds, feelings and consciousnesses of others, those superficialities become meaningless.

During the years that I was raising my daughter JoAnn (now all grown up and mother to my grandchildren) as a single parent, I wanted her to learn to see other human beings as individuals rather than as representatives of groups. In terms of the commonly-held racial stereotypes, I tried to achieve this goal by simply ignoring all references to "race" or ethnicity. She attended a nursery school that had a random mix of children with all different coloration of eyes, hair and skin, and representing a broad diversity of cultural backgrounds. In referring to other children, or *any* other person, I was careful never to use such group-defining words as "white" "black," "Latin," "Asian," etc.

I knew that I had attained some measure of success during those important years of early personality formation when she was talking one day about one of the other children whose name I did not recognize. When I acknowledged that I didn't know who she was talking about, JoAnn said, "Oh, Daddy, you know her. She's about this tall, with dark brown skin, brown eyes, short curly hair and she's very skinny." It never occurred to her to lump various characteristics together under a single catch-all description such as "African American" that would tie her friend to a stereotype. Not until JoAnn entered the public school system, with its well-intentioned emphasis on "awareness" and "support" for various ethnic groups, did she begin to learn commonly-held stereotypes. I hope the perspectives of her early experience allow her to continue to interact with individuals, not stereotypes. As she matured into womanhood and motherhood with a broad range of interests and friends from all backgrounds, I felt I had achieved my objective.

The same concept applies to gender bias. In personal relationships, the traditional "macho" role causes many men to keep a personal distance from women, who are regarded as housekeepers or sex objects, while their male friends are the "buddies" they go out with for a good time. How many close, warm moments of friendship and tender closeness have traditional males denied themselves because they missed the opportunity to share them with the person closest to them? It is true that when perceived stereotypes are eliminated, those who are put down by them will have the most to gain. But those who are "on top" will also profit by the equality they extend to others. While their gains may not be as great, they will be *better* off, not worse; while they may no longer claim the lion's share of economic or personal "spoils," they enjoy a smaller slice of a larger pie. There is more for everyone!

Aside from the way in which prejudices based on superficialities hurt those who are discriminated against, those who hold such prejudices also suffer.

When "white" people try to hold back the progress of "black" people, or men the progress of women, or those who are straight to those who are attracted to others of the same gender, it is true that the "blacks" or women or gays/lesbians suffer the greater loss. But "whites" or males or straights also suffer. Contributions to science, technology, the arts and economic production that could have benefited everyone, are lost when individuals are denied the education, training, self-esteem and resources to make them. How many scientific, medical or technologically wealth-producing innovations do we *not* enjoy today because of past discrimination against the women or minorities who might have invented or discovered them? How many "white" males will die from cancer or heart disease this year because a cure that might have been developed fifty years ago by a "black" or woman or gay who was denied the opportunity to do so?

The same concepts apply equally in all areas of discrimination: against those with different religious beliefs, those from different cultural or ethnic backgrounds, those with different physical abilities or capacities, or those with different sexual orientations. Those of European descent who are confident in their own personal self-worth are not threatened by the equality of those of African, Latin American or Asian ancestry. Men of quality are not threatened by women of equality. Those who are secure and confident in their own sexuality are not threatened by the sexuality of others, which does not affect them in any way. Only those who are weak, insecure or feel inadequate feel threatened by others who differ in ways not relevant to what they are able to contribute for the enrichment of all. When we look beyond the superficial differences and see each person as a unique individual having a special and distinct personality and life story, tensions disappear as we and they are all enriched together.

When human beings see beyond differences in language, culture, gender, sexual orientation, disability or merely the superficiality of physical appearance and embrace the values of others as *individuals*, members of all groups will be enriched.

Chapter 10 Summary
When we see the unique value of every person as an individual, instead of through superficial stereotypes, we expand our opportunities for happiness and avoid the erroneous trap of making judgments based on meaningless or prejudicial characteristics.

11

Social Order and Prosperous Public Policy

We have discussed how compassionate values *enhance* opportunities for personal improvement, individual happiness and contentment, and financial success, while also addressing the legitimate "first step" needs of the self.

But as noted earlier, families, communities and even nations are made up of individuals coming together to address their common interests, and to deal with issues that affect them jointly, beyond what any one individual can achieve on their own.

Size and Role of Government

Too often, we hear the differences between self-described progressives or conservatives as being a choice between more government or less government. The issue is not more government or less government. The issue is good government — big enough to address the legitimate public policy issues that maintain public order, protect individuals and address shared needs of the community, while simultaneously respecting and protecting the privacy and individuality of our personal choices and lifestyles as individuals.

There are some who would demand "smaller government" and demand that government "get off the backs" of corporations and businesses and look the other way when they want to run roughshod over the rights of workers, consumers or cause damage to our shared environment or infrastructure. Yet many of these same people also call on the government to micromanage some of the most personal, intimate decisions of our private lives.

In contrast, there are those who do not want to see Big Intrusive Government (BIG) stick its public nose into private relationships (dictate who you can or can't marry), private medical choices (reproduction, medical marijuana, end of life choices, stem cell therapies) or try to force religion (private) into the public square (socialized religion), or intrude in legitimate free-market commercial or business choices within a protective framework to ensure the rights of workers, consumers and to protect our shared infrastructure and environment.

Most of us can agree that there is a need for "we the people" to come together as "government" through our elected representatives (in a system designed to ensure that such representatives are chosen by real people and not bought off by corporate or other special interests) to address issues that affect the community as a whole, beyond what we are able to address privately or as individuals: matters of emergency disaster response, infrastructure, public order (both proactive [preventive] and reactive [solving problems after they occur]), and protecting the equality of opportunity for all citizens and protecting the interests of the powerless from being dominated by the powerful — to protect consumers, workers, the disadvantaged, the marginalized and our shared environment from threats both domestic (via law enforcement and both our criminal and civil judicial systems) or foreign (via our brave military heroes). Oh, and many who hold such views would also agree that *public policy* also includes *public* health and safety, including health care as public policy, not for the profits of private corporations.

The key is the *"balance between the extremes"* — government that is big enough to play its rightful role, but not so big it intrudes into matters of personal lifestyle preference.

Prosperity for the Greatest Number

What about financial opportunities at the community level — a peaceful, prosperous social order, with public and economic policies to benefit the greatest possible number of people? In all parts of the world, and in all eras of history, economic policies based on greed have failed to generate prosperity. What would be the attributes of an economic policy consistent with the practical compassion of Extro • Dynamics? Compassionate economic policies must:

- bring people from all segments of the economy together, instead of pitting them against each other
- increase accessibility to economic participation for as many people as possible to help address legitimate "first step" needs so as many people as possible can be made ready to move on to higher levels of personal advancement. Prosperity should be as broad-based as possible, not restricted to just a few elites at the top.
- encourage fair and equitable distribution of the wealth produced among all those who participate in producing it, commensurate with the value of their contribution.

To whatever extent possible, these goals should be achieved with a minimum of government intrusion into the personal lives or private economic decisions of individuals. They should rely primarily on positive market forces and incentives to *attract* compliance, but use *reasonable* regulatory controls when needed.

The proposals offered here are one writer's analysis. Others sharing the same values might offer different suggestions. What is most important is that such policies reflect the values of a compassion-based social policy, implemented in a practical way, that both respects the individuality of private, personal preferences while also recognize a balanced approach to legitimate public policy needs.

There are some who would express concern about any public policy involvement in matters of economic policy. There are some who would say that "markets" should be left to themselves, and that the "invisible hand" of market economics (supply and demand) will protect all interests.

Such people often cite Adam Smith, often referred to as the "father of capitalism." Those who cite Adam Smith in order to support a policy of *"laissez-faire"* hands-off deregulation betray their lack of understanding of what Smith actually wrote.

Smith wrote his economic classic, *An Inquiry into the Nature and Causes of the* **Wealth of Nations,** in 1776, the same year that the American founding fathers declared their political independence. Many conservatives wrongly conflate the two. The American founders did not endorse or even make any reference to Smith, capitalism or market economics of any kind. Smith was not part of the American struggle for independence. On the contrary, his 1776 classic was written and published in London, England, where he was a loyal subject of King George III.

Moreover, Smith's model of economic capital markets bears little resemblance to the *"laissez-faire"* economic model that essentially says, "get the government off our backs." The term *"laissez-faire* dates back to a 1736 speech by René de Voyer, Marquis d'Argenson (40 years before "Wealth of Nations"), which a man of Smith's education would surely be familiar with.

Wealth of Nations by Adam Smith is presented in five volumes. My edition contains more than 750 pages, though this may vary depending on page size, type size and other typographical formatting. It does not take five volumes and 750+ pages to say "get the government off our backs."

Public policy oversight does not infringe free market principles. Many who claim to support market economic principles have a tremendous misunderstanding of what market principles are or how they operate. Adam Smith introduced us to the "invisible hand" of market economics based on the balanced interplay of supply and demand.

Smith also understood that it was necessary to have regulatory oversight to protect against the extremes. Smith understood that appropriate regulations do not impede free markets. On the contrary, it makes them possible. Regulation no more limits the free interchange of commerce than rules of the road prevent you from getting in your car and driving anywhere your heart desires, or rules of sports prevent an infinitely unlimited combination of strategies, plays and outcomes such that no two games of any sport have ever been exactly the same. Appropriate regulatory oversight does not impede, it enables and makes possible an infinite range of possible choices and strategies on a level playing field accessible to all. Those who use the excuse of regulatory oversight to explain their failures, while so many around them are succeeding, are possibly not cut out for that role in the first place.

Adam Smith supported progressive tax rate structures, as well as regulation of financial markets, investment markets and capital markets, and public spending for infrastructure and public education, long before it was widely practiced, and in a time prior to industrialization when his nation, like ours, was more rural than urban, and when businesses meant mostly mom-and-pop butchers, bakers and candlestick makers rather than huge industrial corporations or big-box (or online) retail systems of marketing.

Is it possible that, if Adam Smith were to come back today, many of those who invoke his name would call him a socialist?

The Failure of Extremism

Policies rooted in ideological extremes have always failed to deliver economic betterment for *all* participants. Americans are fed up with partisan bickering. They perceive Republicans as helping the rich get richer and Democrats as wasting money on social experiments. On a global level, people reject extremes Communism as well as pure, unregulated capitalism.

In the early 1990's we witnessed the collapse of Communism while, at the same time, un-regulated market economies also failed the test of compassion. While Eastern Europe was throwing off the yoke of Communist domination, and the Soviet empire was dismantled, nations with inadequate protections for workers and consumers in the name of free markets found themselves mired in economic failure, and trying to cope with problems of crime, poverty, homelessness and extremes in the distribution of wealth.

In the United States, during the greed-oriented decade of the 1980's, hostile takeovers, deregulatory strategies favoring investors and leveraged buy-outs in the private sector resulted in a collapse of major markets and financial institutions, weakening the economy. Cutbacks in productivity and innovation caused the United States to lose ground in its technological leadership, resulting in trade deficits, budget deficits and industrial stagnation. Health care became inaccessible to many. Home ownership, virtually taken for granted from the late 1940's to the mid-1970's, became almost impossible for first-time buyers until the market collapsed under its own weight in the late 1980's, while paper wealth equity created a tremendous windfall for those who got in and out of the cycle at opportune times, as inflation in housing galloped at a rate far above general inflation. Poverty, desperation, lack of educational and employment opportunities or mental health services drove increased numbers to drugs, crime and violence. While the middle class shrank and poverty became more widespread, wealth was increasingly concentrated in the hands of a few who benefited greatly — with the result that sales of luxury cars, multi-million dollar homes, expensive artwork and costly electronic toys increased dramatically [Phillips, 1990].·

In third world countries, feudal economies with virtually no industrial regulation resulted in a concentration of most productive resources in the hands of a very small wealthy class while masses of the poor live in urban squalor or in impoverished rural villages. The gap between rich and poor is carried to its farthest extreme.

A Balance Between Extremes

If Communism, capitalism or third-world feudalism all fail to meet community needs, what *does* work? There are success stories: Despite their own ups and downs, Germany and Japan have recovered from the physical, spiritual and economic devastation of military defeat in 1945 to become economic superpowers. The Scandinavian countries are doing quite well. Singapore and Taiwan are still prospering even though, like Japan, they lack adequate land and natural resources. Japan and Germany are free-market economies, right? Mostly. But in both Japan and Germany, industry responds to market demands, yet works closely with government to manage resources and influence distribution of wealth, largely due to social traditions along with regulatory systems imposed on them by Western occupying forces following World War II.

American history also offers a successful economic model. In the 1930's, despite rich natural and land resources, we suffered from the economic devastation of unrestrained free-market policies. But the New Deal, a basic free-market system with moderate regulatory protections for workers, consumers and investors, set in motion an unprecedented economic recovery and prosperity that blossomed into the greatest and most successful economic power-house in any time or place in the history of humankind.

Why did we retreat from this successful model? By the 1970's, the regulatory controls designed to protect us from the extremes had themselves become excessive. Ridiculous examples of bureau-cratic waste, inefficiency and outright corruption became common-place. There were many demands for bureaucratic reform and reduction in the size and scope of government influence. It became necessary to identify and correct legitimate examples of govern-ment excess, institute safeguards against future abuse and adapt programs and policies to meet changing needs. What we got instead was an attempt to completely dismantle all the regulatory protections that had created this prosperity and kept it going for so long. Recession, reduced productivity, and a widening gap between rich and poor are the consequences.

And again, while some may fear that appropriate public policy oversight may infringe the individuality, self-reliance and initiative we championed in Chapter 11, "Achieving Financial Security," as noted earlier, as long as such oversight is limited to the protection of legitimate public policy interests, there is no infringement, and even Adam Smith, the Father of Capitalism, would agree with that.

Even with the ideal of a basic free-enterprise system, with its cornerstone of personal responsibility, not every person is born with equal access to free-market opportunities. It's not just money. It is not necessary to be born with money to become wealthy. There are so many people who were born with nothing, yet became successful that the phrase "rags to riches" has become a cliché. If you take all the money away from a self-made millionaire, he'll quickly earn it all back, as discussed in Chapter 7. The difference between the rich and poor is not just money — it is knowledge, resourcefulness, motivation, "networking" connections and self-confidence. The mere loss of money cannot defeat such wealth.

But children who are born to violence, abuse, crime, drugs and hopelessness, with a constant message of hopelessness and inferiority, will never have the same opportunity to achieve the true potential of their human birthright as those who are born to greater advantage, although some rare, exceptional individuals do overcome such barriers. It is not just a matter of poverty, but a negative perception of themselves and the world that must be reversed and replaced with *positive values.* Since their environment doesn't offer these positive influences, public policy must intervene to provide not equality of results, but equality of opportunity for every participant so that everyone, not just the rare exceptional achievers, can attain such success.

Certainly the primary responsibility for the teaching of values and for providing an environment conducive to readiness for opportunity lies with a child's parents. But if the parents neglect this responsibility, society suffers too much damage in the form of increased crime and economic loss (not to mention interpersonal unhappiness) just to ignore it. With emphasis on *helping the family to assume its proper role,* and helping provide the tools to do so, society must also be prepared to step in as a backup, in a purely secondary role, through its educational and social institutions, as we will discuss in greater depth later in this book.

To summarize:

Socialism: Left wing extremism.
Government owns and micromanages productive resources.
Loves labor; despises investment and administration.
Seeks equality of OUTCOMES.
Perceives liberty and equality as incompatible: exalts equality (of outcomes) and disdains liberty.

Feudalism/Monarchism/Deregulation: Right wing extremism.
Laissez-faire micromanagement of personal morals but economic anarchy and freedom for economic and corporate elites.
Loves investment and administrations; despises, abuses, dominates and oppresses labor.
Does not seek equality. Seeks two-tiered class system where elites dominate subservient class.
Perceives liberty and equality as incompatible: exalts "liberty" (for corporations) and disdains equality.

Classic Liberalism: Balance between the extremes.

Entrepreneurial private sector of free enterprise, with infinite business decisions made within a framework of regulatory protections to prevent harming others such as workers, consumers and the common infrastructure and environment shared with others.

(Workers + Investors + Consumers = Win - win - win

Recognizes that investment/administration and labor must work together for the common benefit of both.

Seeks equality of OPPORTUNITY (level playing field)

Perceives liberty and equality of opportunity (not outcomes) as not only *not* incompatible, but necessarily and inextricably interconnected components of each other.

Compassionate public policy that addresses the underlying causes of hopelessness and poverty must support individual responsibility utilizing practical factors of supply and demand. The goal is to find the middle-ground balance of both "rugged individualism" and a sense of the community's proper role. I call it "Free Market — *Plus*." Let's see how it works....

Fallacies of "Trickle Down" "Supply Side" Economics

Beginning in the 1980's, a model of economic deregulation was based on a theory of "Supply Side" economics developed by Arthur Laffer. The basic idea was that policies of taxation and regulation favoring the wealthiest citizens, who own or control the productive resources, would encourage spending for investment, resulting in an increased "supply" of goods and services and thus a total growth in the economy. A stronger tax base from a larger economic pie would lead to greater income for the government, offsetting the lower tax rates. An increased supply of goods would result in lower costs of those goods, thus benefiting consumers. Increased wealth for investors would "trickle down" to employees. While the wealthy would gain the greatest immediate benefit, the economy as a whole was supposed to grow. Everyone would benefit!

Many proponents of "Supply Side" economics are sincere, well-intentioned and compassionate. Many were very surprised when ambitious tax cuts and economic incentives for the rich, coupled with huge spending increases, resulted in greater deficits than ever before in American history. The assumptions of the "Supply Siders" failed because they were based on several key misunderstandings about how the economy helps or hurts people:

Supply separated from demand. Focus on the "supply-side" of the supply/demand equation attempts to separate supply from demand. The supply side can *only* be considered in conjunction with demand-side factors. Supply side theory tries to set the various economic factors against each other in a counterproductive way. Because the interplay of *both* **supply** *and* **demand**, together, is the basis of Adam Smith's theory of economic capitalism, the attempt to disengage them, and even pit them against each other, could actually be seen as standing up in opposition against Adam Smith and capitalism, ironically by those who most loudly invoke his name! Any compassionate economic theory must bring people together so that all segments of the community — workers, investors, consumers — are pulling together for mutual economic prosperity.

The real demand. So, in the interactive balance between "supply" and "demand," where does the real demand come from? Often, those focused on the supply side dismiss labor — the productive efforts by working people to actually produce goods and services to create real economic wealth — as part of the cost of doing business, like paying for buildings, equipment, supplies and inventory. But unlike other costs of doing business, workers are not objects. Workers are human beings. And as human beings, workers are complex. And in the economic system, they are multidimensional. Yes, they are paid for their productive efforts, and their compensation is part of the cost of doing business. But unlike buildings, equipment, supplies or inventory, workers, in their other roles as actual persons, go out and buy stuff. They buy the stuff they make, as well as other stuff made by other workers in other companies. They recycle the money back into the economy. If everyone is working to produce goods and services and then, using a system of exchange known as "money," redistributing the wealth they all created back to each other, everyone can work, lots of stuff gets created, and there is broad-based general prosperity.

But this only happens if workers are paid a fair share of the real wealth they produce. When workers do not have enough money — enough of their share of the wealth they created — to recycle it back into stimulating the economy, then factories cannot hire workers, unemployment results, and the former workers can no longer to buy goods and services, so others at other companies also lose their jobs, and the economy stagnates such that only a few at the top have wealth, and there not enough business owners, CEOs or investors to create the broad-based demand necessary to sustain a vibrant, prosperous economy.

Making sure that everyone shares in the wealth they help create and is treated fairly is not only the right thing to do, but causes business and economies to thrive.

Misconceptions about "supply." Supply-Siders assume that "supply" is controlled by those who own or manage the productive resources in an economy. If that element could be stimulated, supply would be enhanced. But those who own productive resources mostly just deal in transfers of "paper" wealth — they seldom actually create anything. They merely own and control wealth that is produced by others. This is not to say that their role is not important. On the contrary, they allocate resources and create the environment in which the creation of wealth becomes possible, but they are not the ones who actually create that wealth.

The Real "Supply Side." In order to fully understand the failure of supply-side "Voodoo Economics"[1] we must understand the real nature of the "supply side" of the supply/demand equation, *without separating it from the "demand" side.* "Supply" of goods and services occurs when those goods and services are *produced.* The creation of wealth —"supply"— is not accomplished only by those who buy and sell stocks, trade ownership of real estate or invest in industrial ventures. Such investors have an important role in the management of those resources, but this administrative role cannot be put into conflict with the role of productive labor.

---

[1]"Voodoo Economics" was George Bush's term for supply-side theory while campaigning against Ronald Reagan in the 1980 presidential primary election.

The creation of wealth occurs when raw materials are collected, processed and converted into products, or when services are provided. Cars are not made when investors transfer shares of GM, but when workers go into the mines, gather and process steel, and hammer it into shape. Real estate value is created not only when investors acquire dwellings to rent out or for speculative resale, but when construction laborers transform raw land and materials into homes. Health care value is not just created by those who own hospitals, but by health care professionals who treat patients.

The "supply-side" theory is that if you give tax breaks to the rich or otherwise put more money into the pockets of those who already have the most, that they will use it to create jobs, and the flow of wealth will "trickle down" to those at the bottom. While it is primarily the wealthy that invest the capital needed to create more wealth (and jobs), jobs are not created just because people have money. If they just have money, and that's all, they'll just keep it or spend it on themselves, as they always have done in the past. Jobs are not created as acts of charity for working people that the wealthy elites don't even have personal acquaintance with. Jobs (and broad-based wealth) are created when those in a position to administer productive resources see a *demand* for goods to be produced.

If potential investors do see such a demand (or envision new products for which they believe they can create demand), they will generate the increased production — create new jobs — *whether or not they have the money on hand* — even if they have to raise money by borrowing the necessary capital for financing. Many small startup businesses began with money borrowed from parents, friends or put on credit cards because someone had a vision and believed they could satisfy an existing demand or create a new one.

But if the general public, which is made up far ore by working people than by the wealthy elite, does not have discretionary income to spend on products or services, the broad-based demand needed to stimulate wealth creation (and job creation) is inhibited. It has more to do with creating a broad base of demand than by making sure rich people have enough money.

162

Thus we see again that, in the economic process, *supply cannot be separated from demand*. The real supply of goods is stimulated by the real demand for goods. As Adam Smith predicted, supply and demand are just flip sides of the same economic coin.

Stimulating the real supply side requires economic incentives for the real producers (workers) as well as the investors, in policies consistent with universal compassion for all contributors. Wealth does not "trickle down," but it bubbles up with a rising tide that lifts all boats together, in the words of John F. Kennedy.[1] And tides lift from below; they don't "trickle down" from above.

Socialist economies fail because they offer no *incentive* for workers to actually produce. Restaurant servers are paid the same whether cheerful and prompt or slow and surly; workers in factories or farms are paid whether efficient or incompetent; managers are paid no matter how much or little they contribute to increased production. The only incentive is to do as little as possible and not "rock the boat." Perhaps the failure of Socialism has more to do with the lack of incentives than with the attempt to operate a centrally-managed system. (The one area in which Eastern block nations *did* incorporate strong incentives, yet which remained centrally managed, was their competitive sports program. In this venture, even small, troubled nations such as Romania and East Germany were able to achieve dramatic successes.)

By the same token, in totally-deregulated economies favoring those who own productive resources, the incomes and benefits of owners, investors and top-level managers skyrocket, while those on the front lines who create real wealth must endure cutbacks in pay. This is not a *consequence* of the recession, but a *cause*, as productive incentives are reduced. It is also not compassionate.

When taken to the furthest extreme, in third-world economies where there are *no* protections for workers, there is no incentive to

---

[1] The expression that "a rising tide lifts all boats" originates from remarks made by John F. Kennedy at the dedication of a public works project (Greers Ferry Dam in Heber Springs, Arkansas; October 3, 1963) that continued the prosperity-generating policies of infrastructure and publicly-stimulated employment that had lifted us out of the Great Depression and had continued through the Eisenhower administration's extensive public works projects.

produce beyond mere survival. The economy becomes totally stagnant, resulting in widespread poverty and squalor. Beggars, thieves or throngs of impoverished workers earning subsistence wages crowd the streets. Some say they are lazy. Yet the beggars, hustlers and thieves start early in the morning and stick with it all day, every day. Survival is hard work. Those who do have jobs work fiercely to keep them, even at poverty wages, knowing there are many who are even more desperate, ready to take their places.

Spending the windfall. 1980's deregulators assumed that the wealthy would invest their extra money back into the economy. But by making the rich richer and everyone else poorer, they set one class against the other and hurt everyone. There was no "trickle down." As tax rates at the top plummeted in the 1980's and again in the first decade of the 21st Century, the rich did not invest their windfall in jobs — *they kept it.* Narrowly-focused elite sales of exotic autos, high-priced electronic gadgets, expensive fine arts, jewelry, fashions, and high-tech toys (purchased by a small elite) increased dramatically, while more broad-based sales to the general public of middle-class autos, household appliances and everyday goods (previously purchased by many) plummeted and workers on the assembly line saw a steady decline in their paychecks. Purchases of expensive homes climbed exponentially, as did the acquisition of rental holdings (previously owned by the people who lived in them), while the number of owner-occupied dwellings fell.

The money was spent in a smaller economic circle. Even the workers who found jobs creating those elite products saw a larger share of the money from those sales going to the small circle of owner/investors instead of to themselves as the general pool of lower-paid workers and consumers, turned toward a two-tiered economy with an income gap separating the rich and everyone else. Because of regulatory protections remaining in place, the United States did *not* become a two-tiered economy like those in third-world countries, but began taking small steps in that direction. Supply-side theory provides no incentives to guarantee adequate wages or benefits to workers. There was little compassion in the economy of the 1980's.

Models for Success

In the 1930's, following two decades of failed economic policies pitting investors, consumers and workers against each other, the United States found itself in a Depression with squalid conditions similar to what we now see in the third-world. Government spending didn't help. Many forget that Herbert Hoover, a fiscal conservative, spent more for economic recovery than any previous president. But, like modern Supply-siders, incentives were aimed at *investors*. A few profited, while many others remained poor. It was the New Deal of the next administration, with federal spending to create jobs and protect the productive work force, that ended the Depression. It was not just "government spending," but *spending to benefit the productive sector,* leading to 45 years of uninterrupted prosperity. Similarly, in Japan, productivity is encouraged with a system of unprecedented protection and incentives for workers and cooperation between business and government, in a partnership that Ross Perot calls "21st Century Capitalism."

Could this work in the third world? Perhaps there is no place in the world where poverty is more severe than in Bangladesh. As widely reported, Harvard-trained economist Muhammad Yunus (who was awarded the 2006 Nobel Peace Price) was frustrated in his attempts to help impoverished workers. He tells of a woman who was paid 2¢ a day for her skillful weaving of exquisite baskets that sold in the market for much more than that. But because the woman could not raise enough capital from her subsistence wages to pay a mere six dollars for her own equipment and supplies to make a basket, she could not break free from the grip of poverty. Yunus was tempted to give her the six bucks and be on his way, but realized that giving $6 to one woman would not solve the widespread poverty. So he *loaned* her the $6 at 16% interest, to be paid back from the higher earnings of her economic self-sufficiency. With this loan, the woman became financially secure. This experience led Yunus to establish the Grameen Bank, which has since made small loans to *millions* of impoverished Bangladeshis. The model, now called "micro credit" is now being replicated by others, including the World Bank, and with its incentives for real production, addresses underlying causes of poverty with compassion and dignity for those most in need. Further, because

165

the loans are repaid at a 98% rate and with the interest charges for the loans, the Grameen Bank has not only rescued thousands from poverty, it is also profitable and has demonstrated yet again that endeavors to improve the lives of the poor can also be successful commercial ventures. In the long run, altruistic and self interests ultimately converge. The program is so successful that billionaire investors such as Bill Gates and others have established similar self-funding programs in impoverished third-world countries. [Counts, 1996]

A Tale of Two Post-World War II Island Nations: Several decades ago, I was riding in a car in the Philippines, where I have many close relatives and friends. We were riding in Metro Manila, along a lengthy road named Epifanio del los Santos Avenue, or EDSA for short, that forms a ring around the cities that form Metro Manila. As was common, the street was lined with the poor beggars, desperately seeking some small morsel of food or cash with which to survive another day in a nation with virtually no social safety net.

I contemplated how a nation of people who were so hard working could also have so many living in squalid poverty. I tried to consider the historical origins of such poverty. What is now the Republic of the Philippines was originally a chain of more than 7,000 islands with island people of Malay stock representing a number of diverse communities and peoples, with a variety of languages, cultures and traditions. These people lived happy and free, much like many other indigenous peoples of Pacific island nations, until conquered by the Spanish beginning with the invasion of Ferdinand Magellan, who was killed on Mactan Island, Cebu. Two monuments stand at that site, side-by-side in unflinching irony, = in the same province where many of my close relatives and friends still live today, honoring both Magellan, for introducing Christianity, and Lapu Lapu, the islander who killed him, as the first blow, however futile, against European imperialism. [Manchester, pp. 267-286]

After centuries of Western colonial domination, first by the Spanish and then by the United States (which some have described as 300 years in a convent followed by 50 in a brothel), the

Philippines was granted independence, and put on an economically conservative policy agenda, which benefactor and still-popular hero Douglas MacArthur believed would afford them the greatest opportunity for economic advancement and prosperity.

I considered two island nations, and imagined a scene from September of 1945, aboard the USS Missouri as the United States accepted the formal surrender of the Empire of Japan. Two island nations — the Philippines and Japan. One, the Philippines, had been a close American ally and shared in victory; the other devastated by crushing war including the dropping of two atomic bombs. One, the Philippines, in a tropical climate, was rich in natural resources; the other, a largely rocky, overcrowded island largely dependent on imports. But Douglas MacArthur, who had grown up in the Philippines when his own father, Arthur MacArthur, had been an American commanding governor over the islands, loved the Philippines and wanted them to enjoy a deregulated free market of the kind he believed would lead to prosperity. In contrast, he hated the Japanese, who he had been fighting against for years and who had brutalized and tortured his men as well as innocent civilians. He would not go so far as to impose on them the form of socialized government he equally detested, but he would impose on them a market system subject to strict regulatory oversight and safeguards. He's shown them!

If someone had been standing on the deck of the USS Missouri in September of 1945, and saw the Filipinos standing side-by-side with the Americans in celebratory victory, accepting the unconditional surrender of a crushed and defeated Japan, it would have been inconceivable to predict that, decades later, despite the best intentions of General MacArthur, the Japanese would become one of the great economic powerhouses of the world while the Philippines languished in squalid poverty and widespread economic inequality, with wealth concentrated in the hands of a very few who are very rich while many go begging in the streets.

So as I rode along EDSA, passing the beggars and shanty towns interspersed with scattered luxury tracts and gleaming office high rises, as pockets of wealth seemed to mock the "huddled masses yearning to breathe free" of economic inequality, I considered, what would it take to break the cycle of poverty?

The reason there is so much poverty amid a wealth of natural resources is because the beggars are standing along EDSA instead of going to work and taking those raw materials and turning them into houses, cars, computers and domestic appliances. And why don't they do that? Because there needs to be some mechanism in coordinating the effort to match workers with resources to create products and then distribute them to all the people who worked together to make them so that everyone has enough and no one is in poverty.

The problem is that there is no one who will invest in the startup costs of capitalizing the ventures needed to start that, because workers in the Philippines are poorly paid and companies do not pay working people enough so that they would actually be able to buy back there share of the wealth they create (the local paper, the *Manila Bulletin,* had carried an article that very morning about how the national senate had rejected, yet again, a minimum wage bill). So workers don't get paid enough to buy what they make, there is no one to sell to so no one to produce for, so it just doesn't get done and no one gets the wealth because no one produces it because there are not enough consumers to buy it.

Solutions? Some suggest just having the public come together to do it as a community, *i.e.,* communally or via socialism. Others are apprehensive about government running the economy, and prefer market solutions. Clearly, as we saw in the difference in outcomes between the Philippines and Japan, viable solutions can come through market economics, but with public policy intervention to smooth out and provide oversight for the processes of capitalization, administration and implementing policies to protect workers and consumers (who are the same people, but who play multiple roles in the economic performance) so that workers can produce and, in their role as consumers, can also buy with confidence to create domestic markets.

Public Capitalization for *Private* Enterprise. A proposal that takes the Grameen Bank concept even further might entail some role of the government in funding the capitalization of larger industrial operations (such as factories for heavy machinery, high-tech electronics, solar energy or zero-emission automobiles), providing good jobs at good wages (production coupled with the enhancement of a domestic market of consumers), and then sell them back to the workers as employee-owned cooperatives. This would allow private-sector investments and profit incentives to go directly to the workers who create the wealth, effectively combining ownership, investment and production.

In third world countries, such a proposal would allow the government to stimulate, but not own or operate, private industry while using the terms of the charter to spell out favorable standards for wages, environmental standards and consumer protection that other industrial firms would then have to compete with, generating widespread economic growth in a compassionate framework.

In industrialized free-market economies, such a proposal would allow the government a mechanism for moderating shifts in markets, such as when an obsolete industry is being phased out or military contracts are being scaled back. The government could capitalize new industries that require help in getting established, concentrating in areas hardest hit by economic or social shift, setting standards for wages, employee safety, and protection for consumers and the environment, putting competitive pressure on other firms as an alternative form of industrial regulation. Yet the intervention would always be transitory, because the very act of chartering the cooperative would spell out, from the beginning, the terms of its transfer back to the private sector. Truly, "Free Market — *Plus!*"

A note about inflation: While long-range economic strength depends on a broad base of high-wage, productive employment, in the short run wages cannot be increased too rapidly. If the supply of money is drastically increased at a rate too far ahead of increased productive output, there will be too much money and not enough goods to buy with it. This imbalance between supply and demand of money causes inflation. In the short run, inflation must be countered in two ways: first, tying any increase in the total money supply to commensurate increases in total productivity; and second, indexing prices, wages, fees and public benefits as broadly as possible, so that, to whatever extent any price adjustments do occur, they will be distributed evenly.

The long run solution for inflation, of course, is an economy built on a foundation of full employment at maximum productivity. Putting everyone to work creates a strong *supply* of labor, resulting in downward pressures against excessive wage increases after adequate levels of compensation have been reached so that those who produce goods and services can also afford to buy them. Beyond that, further wage increases are not necessary because full productivity creates an abundant *supply* of available goods and services, keeping prices as low and as stable as possible.

Including "Demand Side" Factors. Socialist systems fail because consideration of demand factors is not directly linked to decisions about production, which are determined by central planning committees. Similarly, Supply-Siders fail when they seek to separate supply from demand in the economic equation. It is demand from consumers, which stimulates production by real producers. And who are these consumers? Everyone in the economy! But since the productive work force is the largest single segment, the same individuals who actually produce wealth (supply) are the largest single component in creating demand for it. *Demand is stimulated when the real producers become the consumers.*

The overall success attributed to free-market economies is the result of the close link between supply and demand. Demand creates supply. Industries will produce what consumers will buy. But it is not an impotent demand of *wishes,* rather a demand based on actual sales. If consumers (mostly from the productive work force) cannot afford to become a potent demand-side buying force, the economy becomes stagnant and everyone suffers.

In the 1930's, when the productive work force enjoyed protections which enabled creation of the supply-side, the same consumer force also developed the economic clout to generate demand, which generated further supply, and so on. As long as those who produce the goods can afford to purchase what they create, a domestic market is created and a cycle of economic prosperity ensues. As New Deal protections were solidified over the next four decades, our economy became increasingly prosperous and the gap between rich and poor steadily narrowed. Only in the last decade, under deregulation, have these gains been reversed. Wages for workers decrease, while salaries at the top skyrocket. The rich get richer. There is less buying power (demand) from the labor force (producers/consumers). The economy slows down.

The old economic truism asserts that the economy prospers during a "wartime economy." Why is that? Why should an economic boom result from diverting productive resources *away from* the production of consumer goods and services, towards products such as bombs and bullets that *destroy* real wealth? Because a massive redistribution of payments is suddenly diverted away from top-level salaries and profits, towards legions of soldiers (consumers), generally recruited from the bottom levels of the economic strata.

Why shouldn't we have, instead, a "wartime economy" based on productive rather than destructive expenditures, in which good jobs are provided at good wages for building roads, hospitals, housing and manufacturing resources under regulatory controls to prevent the balance of wealth from becoming unbalanced — concentrated in favor of those who own and control such resources as the economy sags into a top-heavy recession.

This is the essence of "Free Market — *Plus*": to use free market incentives in private enterprise, with just enough government intervention and regulation to balance out the extremes and bring the interests of owners, investors, workers and consumers together in harmony — a compassionate approach that benefits everyone.

In the extreme example of third-world feudalism, we can see this even more dramatically. If we could take all the hard-working survivalists off the streets and put them in factories producing televisions, autos, appliances, food, and housing, there would be more than enough increased wealth to go around. It wouldn't matter whether those factories were capitalized by private investors, charities, the government, or any combination.

So why *don't* we put them all in factories? Because, under raw capitalism, if they work in a factory, competitive pressures among the investors who own the productive resources will cause them to be paid as little as possible. This means just enough to survive on. If one owner raises salaries, it is not enough to make a dent in the system, and they reduce their competitive edge in pricing against those who continue to pay the lower salaries. No single investor has the economic clout to go first, so the productive work force does not have enough money to buy the products they could have been producing. There is no mechanism for distributing the wealth that could have been created, so there is no incentive to actually take the laborers off the street and make them productive. The people remain poor, while the investors miss out on a great opportunity. The vicious cycle can only be broken when the community as a whole, through government, establishes minimum standards to protect workers and consumers, reflecting its compassion.

In theory, the deregulatory *laissez-faire* interpretation of Adam Smith's theory of the "Invisible Hand" of capitalism is supposed to regulate such excesses, as workers exercise their "economic freedom" to enter into voluntary contracts with investors, exchanging labor for money. But in practice, there is no "free market" if both sides do not have reasonably equal bargaining positions. Many are surprised to learn that, in developing his theory of capitalism and the creation of wealth, Smith did anticipate that, without safeguards, unbridled greed would lead to harmful excesses. While his theory encourages wealth building through the private sector, it does not advocate the economic anarchy of total deregulation. The massive multi-volume tome includes extensive recommended regulatory guidelines to protect a broad range of social interests and distribute a general economic prosperity as broadly as possible [Smith, 1776].

In completely unregulated feudal economies, where wealth is concentrated in the hands of a few, wealthy elites, agreements between those who own and control resources, and the laborers and consumers who make up the broader community, are based to a large extent on duress: workers have to take what is offered or die from starvation and exposure; consumers do not have the option of "buyer beware" but rather only of "take it or leave it." The economic imbalance inherent in feudal systems is perpetuated by force, just as it was created and imposed primarily by force.

In the European "Middle Ages," those who had military power in an age of ongoing warfare could offer protection to those who would pledge them fealty and enter into the safety of their castles in exchange for "voluntarily" becoming their subjects. This "social contract," passed on through succeeding generations, became the basis for the "divine right" of kings, although failure to accept such "voluntary" terms of extortion would have meant certain death. Similarly, in the Southern United States prior to emancipation, great wealth was created for plantation owners by workers (slaves) who did not even enjoy a token gesture of "free choice." Although that wealth was passed on by inheritance to succeeding generations, any attempt to restore portions of such wealth to the heirs of its creators has always been labeled "reverse discrimination." In nations victimized by colonial oppression, such as in India, Africa and the Philippines, invaders conquered native populations and expropriated the land and its wealth that was, again, passed on through inheritance to succeeding generations even after the end of colonial rule. Yet those who have inherited unearned wealth in these modern feudal economies still refuse to accept economic reforms to restore any portion of such wealth to the heirs of those from whom it was taken by force, who are still forced to accept an unequal economic contract, with a result of widespread poverty.

Raw, unregulated free-markets do not work. Socialism also doesn't work. We need a balance between the extremes — a basic free-market system, with supply and demand incentives, but with adequate regulation to protect workers and consumers in a compassionate way. Policies of greed, or incentives of taxation that favor a few wealthy instead of the general population of producer / consumers, are counter-productive.

Those on the extreme political right wing worship deregulation like a dogmatic religion, while those on the extreme left would like to throw out the free market altogether. Sensible people see a balance in the middle. We can compare it to sex: sex is the basis of life and free enterprise is the basis of economic life. Both are powerful motivational forces. Long-range sexual satisfaction is maximized within the boundaries of stable relationships, not by just letting the sexual impulse run wild and unrestrained. Similarly, the free market can be destructive when it runs wild and unrestrained, causing extremes of poverty and wealth, and allowing those who own and control productive resources to shut out those who do not and manipulate market forces to gain an unfair advantage over workers and consumers. Reasonable limitations on the *excesses* of capitalism do not diminish the legitimate operation of free markets any more than rules of the road hurt the safe use of automobiles. Appropriate rules and regulations do not inhibit private enterprise, but rather enhance it and expand its range of possibilities. Rules of the road do not stop us from driving; they make it possible and, within those rules, we can get into our cars and go wherever we want. Rules of football or baseball don't bring those games to a halt; they define the boundaries that make those sports possible and within which an infinite range of strategies is possible. Similarly, appropriate regulations do not stop businesses, but rather define the boundaries within which an infinite range of business choices and strategies can be pursued — as long as they do not harm workers, consumers or the environment we all share.

Fiscally Responsible Compassion

The common solutions for today's most pressing social problems lie in policies that are *consistent with* personal and public standards of compassion (without trying to *compel* compassionate feelings nor legislating personal morality). But "compassion" does not necessarily require grandiose and expensive bureaucracies. In the 1960's, during the "Great Society," combined federal and state taxes for Americans of average income were much less than today. Yet the government was able to provide *more* programs and services, with budget deficits a fraction of today's (and even budget surpluses in some states). But today, despite budget-cutting efforts, we pay more taxes for fewer services.

The old saying goes, "If you give a man a fish, you feed him today; if you *teach him to fish,* you feed him for a lifetime." We need less of giving out fishes, and more of *teaching* skills and attitudes to those who have missed out on nurturing growth opportunities so they will not only survive, but prosper, and with a better life for themselves and a more productive economy for everyone.

"Programs" which invest in developing productive human potential do not cause deficits. While examples of outright waste and fraud need to be cut [Gross, 1992; Gore, 1993], the real solution goes much deeper. Even many good programs are riddled with layers of fat (inefficiency, waste, counterproductive incentives to claim entitlements, top-heavy management and corruption) that could be cut. The government is like a fat man whose doctor tells him to lose twenty pounds. He eats another plate of bacon and cuts off a leg. Instead of merely deciding whether to cut or keep existing programs in the budget, we should ask *why* the program costs so much, and how we can cut back the fat while maintaining the same or better service. Because politicians are protective of "pork-barrel" waste that benefits their special interests and constituents, whenever they are cornered with the need for cutting government costs, they scare away the reformers by threatening to reduce or eliminate essential services, like police patrols or trash pickup, instead of the real budgetary reform process that's really needed.

Real budgetary reform, to allow enough money for the operation of government in its proper but limited role, consistent with compassionate public policy, must include the following measures: 1) we must require spending priorities that favor *preventing* rather than *solving* problems; 2) we must mandate maximum levels of administrative overhead; and, 3) we must replace the built-in negative incentives of "base-line budgeting" with positive incentives that favor more prudent spending.

Proactive spending priorities. In order to return to the more efficient days when we spent less and got more for our money, we must again pay for less expensive programs to *prevent* problems (education, mental health, early childhood training, adequate minimum wages and relief for poverty and hopelessness), instead of more expensive programs to solve them *after* they occur (jails, law enforcement, and drug enforcement).

I witnessed a dramatic example of this through my work with Deaf people. One day I got a call to help out with a 20-year-old youth who had gone to a recovery house for drug addicts, asking for help. If he had money or insurance, a private hospital bed would have been available. They told him that, on an emergency basis, they could have a bed open as soon as six days. But when an addict is standing there saying, "Please, help me," six days might as well be a lifetime. By tomorrow he might no longer be in the mood for help. Of course, six days later he was nowhere to be found. The next time I saw that young man was several months later, when I got a call from the jail after he had been arrested for a burglary to support his drug habit. In the middle of America's "War on Drugs," one of the "enemy" wanted to voluntarily surrender and we didn't have the money to help him. How much more do you think it cost for the police, courts and jails, not to mention costs to a victim and to the lost soul of a young deaf man, than if we had just helped him the first time he asked?

I've also seen the reverse — the successes when we *did* help. A couple years later, I got another request to help out a different 20-year-old fellow. He had one foot in the gangs, associating with people encouraging a deeper involvement in drugs and crime. We got him into an adult education program, followed by job training and job placement. With improved self-esteem based on real accomplishments and confidence that he had viable, positive alternatives, he was able to choose a better direction for his life. Those services cost money, but we didn't have to pay the higher costs of less desirable future consequences. Today, he is a happy, productive member of the workforce who contributes to his community.

Limiting administrative overhead. Levels of administrative overhead in the public sector are many times what free-market competition allows for private businesses or charities. We must develop strict definitions of the differences between overhead and front-line services. Required budget cuts to meet spending limits would *necessarily* cut salaries or personnel from administrative staff (by attrition or by reassignment to front-line service duties) until target ratios were achieved, before any services could be cut.

Positive incentives to save. Current base-line budgeting policies encourage waste and inefficiency. If an agency doesn't spend its entire budget, next year's budget will be reduced accordingly. In order to trim the *fat* from the budget, incentives to conserve must be written into all funding measures. In the private sector, the profit motives provide such incentives. We need similar positive incentives in the public sector. For employees, monetary rewards based on a percentage of savings for cost-cutting suggestions would encourage them to reveal where much of the fat his hidden. For managerial and administrative staff, salaries should be cut by a substantial amount, and replaced with bonus options tied to a combination of budget reductions and service performance levels. People who work in public-sector offices know where they've padded the budgets. In the present system, they've had little choice if they wanted to survive. But with a revised system of incentives aimed at their own pockets, you'll be surprised how fast they cut budgets to earn bonuses!

Long range solutions. The budget can only be cut so far by "cutting back," because of "safety net" payments guaranteed by law. The way to reduce costs for "entitlements" (welfare, Social Security, Medicare, etc.) is not to cut people off and throw them out into the street, but rather to offer attractive alternatives for real personal development. When people have a good educational foundation and access to job training in an economy that offers *good* jobs to the productive sector, they enrich society instead of draining its resources. The most practical approaches for long-range solutions demonstrate how all our resources — law enforcement plus education plus social services — must work together, in ways that are compassionate as well as fiscally responsible.

"No man is an island." As with the seemingly contradictory paradox of happiness itself on which Extro • Dynamics is based, economic policies that perpetuate poverty do not benefit the rich. We all pay the price, in a sluggish economy and the higher costs of side effects such as crime and economic squalor. Just as personal policies of compassion promote the opportunities for personal wealth, so also do public policies consistent with the compassion of "Free Market — *Plus"* strengthen the overall economy.

Chapter 11 Summary
Public policies based on the *practical* compassion of Extro•
Dynamics, avoiding ideological extremes, are those that allow the greatest number of people to achieve economic prosperity.

12

Crime

How would a compassionate society deal with the problems of crime and violent behavior? Do we direct our compassion to those who commit crimes or the victims of those crimes?

These problems are serious and devastating, and seem to be getting worse. Politicians and government officials have tried to "get tough" on crime by putting more police on the streets, building more prisons and seeking tougher sentences for criminals, and paying for it by cutting back social programs. Now, with more cops on the street than ever, higher costs for law enforcement, a gridlocked judicial system and jails so crowded that criminals are being released early, there is also more crime, more violence, more gangs and more substance abuse than ever.

We do have to "get tough" on crime. But that means more than just *talking* tough. Real toughness requires a *comprehensive* approach. We need to *prevent* problems, not just clean up after the consequences. As stated before, we must put the fence at the top of the cliff, not just ambulances and coroners at the bottom. We must protect victims by removing dangerous criminals from the streets. But if our society produces criminals faster than we can build the prisons to hold them in, we will spend tremendous sums of money on police and jails, while the problem just gets worse.

The government exists to settle disputes and maintain the public order. Government (the community as a whole, acting through its elected representatives) only exists to prevent people from hurting others. One strategy is to maintain order by enforcing laws after crimes have occurred, which emphasizes police and military solutions. Long-range strategies for maintaining order must also include preventive measures, which are more effective in terms of both costs and results. If serious, well-funded preventive measures are developed and perfected, crime rates will plummet. In the long run, it will cost less, and our "tough" talk on crime can be backed up with *results*.

Policies of cutting back on education, early childhood training, drug and alcohol treatment, detection and prevention of domestic violence and correction of social and economic inequities in order to buy more police officers and jails are short sighted. If people do not have enough self esteem, education, and confidence in having an equal chance at economic opportunities, their feelings of frustration, hopelessness and desperation will grow and fester until they explode in criminal rage and violence. If children grow up in environments of abuse and cruelty, without access to services for reversing those influences, they will perpetuate the cycles of vio-lence, which are the only thing they know.

When shortsighted politicians talk about simply cutting welfare benefits to the poor or educational services for undocumented children, what do they think will happen to these people if they offer no replacement options? Do they think that undocumented children, out of school and on the streets, will just disappear? Can you imagine all these young people on the streets, with nothing to do and no way to earn an honest wage (without documents)? Can anyone seriously believe that such proposals will result in *less* crime, drugs and gangs?

Most of those in prisons are also victims — of squalor, hopelessness and abuse. While we busily punish them, their rates of crime, drug abuse and gang violence keep going up. Their unfortunate experiences do not relieve them of responsibility for their adult decisions, but it demonstrates that a society unwilling to address *all* causes of victimization will suffer new generations of victims, distributed in patterns both predictable (their own families and neighborhoods) and random (anyone else they victimize).

Solving the *causes* of crime requires a compassionate response, not only as individuals, but as a society. It is not the role of society to *force* people to become compassionate, but public policy must be based on public values that are at least consistent with public compassion. Ironically, such policies are also the most effective.

School systems must provide formal instruction in self-esteem, social values and interpersonal relations skills as part of the public curriculum, starting in kindergarten, and taught in conjunction with other subjects. While the responsibility to teach values rests first with parents, it becomes a public matter when the parental role is neglected, causing children to grow up in violence and cruelty to themselves and others. (See Chapter 14, "Teaching Children.")

We must make sure *everyone* has equal access to educational and economic opportunities. Special needs must be addressed to remove any obstacles to equal opportunity as part of our comprehensive strategy to prevent rather than cure problems of crime, violence and substance abuse. Not only is it the *right thing to do,* but it will also result in lower costs in the long run.

We must teach young people early, and not wait until they have become full-blown criminals. We not only need more youth activities, family services and early rehabilitative intervention, but our *comprehensive* strategy also requires a stronger early response to "minor" offenses such as vandalism, graffiti, cruelty to animals, noise or truancy. Instead of treating these offenses lightly, we must recognize the danger signals and intervene aggressively (but compassionately) to make sure that these "petty crimes" do not blossom into serious patterns of habitual criminal activity.

Even with a strong barrier at the top of the cliff, some cars will manage to get through. We will always need good "ambulance" services. Our *comprehensive* approach requires strong law enforcement, and we will always need prisons for those who can't adjust in society. But these should be the back up, not the first line of defense. With good, *preventive* programs, those expensive "after-the-fact" solutions can be greatly reduced.

When crimes are committed, our compassion for victims demands that criminals must be dealt with firmly, but also compassionately. In our institutional dealings with criminals, we must remember the lessons from Chapter 6, "Lifestyle Situations," about dealing with negative interactions at the personal level, and apply them to social policy: we can feel compassion for criminals while taking forceful action to stop their destructive behavior.

When desperate, hopeless individuals express their rage and frustration in ways that hurt others, we must respond with strong measures that unmistakably say, "No!" We must make sure that criminals are removed from the conditions that spawned them, which requires that they lose the freedom they can't control.

Just as individual victims of crimes can use compassion to break free of their assailants' control over their feelings, societies can do the same. Most prisoners will eventually be returned to society. If we merely perpetuate the cruelty they have already experienced, their time in prison is wasted. It will only make them more cruel, and perhaps more skilled in their vicious trades.

It is crucial that, when criminals have proven their inability to handle personal freedom and have had it taken from them, we use the time we have them in our custody to reverse the influences of cruelty that have shaped their lives. Perhaps many are beyond our ability to help them. But in the present system we will never know, because there has never been a thorough effort to address the personal development that they didn't get earlier. Psychologists today understand the basic hierarchy of needs that must be met for positive personality development. We know how to provide help to those willing or able to pay adequate sums for personal therapy. As described earlier, these criminals are often the victims we were unable to identify and help as children. We should feel loathing and fear for their criminal behavior, and take all measures to stop it, yet respond with compassion to them as individuals. But we have never had a concerted institutional effort to provide for the basic nurturing needs of those in our care. On a small scale, some individuals and private organizations have tried to address those needs and have found remarkable success in turning around the seemingly hopeless, desperate lives of these former victims. Past efforts at "rehabilitation" have been small and superficial. We need a real commitment to prepare prisoners for eventual release, as most will be. We must provide education, job training, job placement assistance and personal development skills and values — not as an afterthought, but as the primary focus of institutional care.

Use of prisoners to provide labor in many areas of government service, administrative, clerical and hard labor, would provide them opportunities to get work experience while saving taxpayers the tremendous costs of public-sector salaries, thus helping to pay the costs of meeting prisoner needs.

Those who seem to respond to rehabilitation should not necessarily be rewarded with shorter sentences. Perhaps that would only encourage them to feign progress. In any case, there are many other incentives that can be offered to motivate good behavior, such as access to recreational facilities, higher levels of trust and responsibility within the institutional setting, etc. Nor am I saying that we can always reverse deeply-rooted failures developed from the very beginnings of personality formation. But we should seek whatever success is possible, which would be better than the current policy. Despite tougher sentencing guidelines, most criminals will be released at some point. Any improvement, no matter how small, would afford greater security to society when it is time to return these criminals/victims to the general public. If we would really apply current psychological knowledge to meet unsatisfied needs, we could go a long way towards reclaiming the tortured lives of those who now cause only pain to themselves and their innocent victims, and preventing harm to future victims.

A comprehensive, compassion-based strategy should also include substantial reform and streamlining of the judicial process. Right now, there is tremendous waste of time and money for convoluted motions, repeat appearances and inefficient procedures. Working in the courts to assist with the needs of non-English speaking defendants and litigants, I have seen first hand the waste and bureaucracy of the courtroom process, which often exists only to satisfy arcane traditions, judicial egos or drive up fees for attorneys, with the result that many are denied equal access to the justice system. Those who rely on dedicated but overworked public defenders do not receive the same justice as those who can afford very expensive legal representation. Procedures should be made much less formal, similar to binding arbitration in the civil courts: the parties benefit from informal yet efficient processes which, without injury to their rights, saving time and money and ensuring that justice is more swift and sure — and compassionate.

The same principles apply in handling negative situations at the community level as the individual level (See Chapter 6). Real justice occurs when we "love our enemies," without tolerating their evil behavior. We must treat those who victimize us the same as we would treat our own children or loved ones if they were to victimize others: stop the bad behavior (removing them from normal society if necessary); personal development (skills and values education); and appropriate disciplinary justice.

We must reject "compassion" as an excuse for letting others take advantage of us. We must *prevent* problems. We must take *action* that is both practical and compassionate to stop destructive behavior and overcome the early influences that cause it.

Community strategies based on compassion, addressing the needs of individuals from the perspectives of their own unique situations, represent the ultimate solution for both preventing and solving the problems of crime and violence.

Chapter 12 Summary

Comprehensive, compassion-based strategies for controlling crime and violence must forcefully stop criminal behavior and get criminals off the streets, with emphasis on preventing the *causes* of antisocial behavior and criminal violence, while also rehabilitating criminals before they are returned to the mainstream population.

13

Competitiveness

I love sports. My particular favorite is baseball. I grew up in Los Angeles, rooting for the Dodgers who moved there when I was just seven. I traded baseball cards and chewed more bubble gum than I would like to recall. In high school, I went out for the freshman team and, though no great athlete, I only lettered because our team tied for the championship. And there are more hours than I would care to confess to when I spent my afternoons watching ball games when I should have been doing something more industrious.

But in the late 1960's, after I had developed the beginnings of what would become Extro • Dynamics, I began trying to make it a part of my own life. When applied to *competitive sports,* I made an interesting discovery. The first time I noticed it was on a summer's evening at Dodger Stadium in 1970. As I was watching and enjoying the game, I ran through the four steps in rapid succession in my interactions, however briefly, with others that I passed in the crowd going to and from my seat, in the lines at concessions, and near where I was sitting. As always, the magic worked well, drawing me beyond the limitations of self-concern and adding new dimensions to my enjoyment of a night out at the ballpark.

Even as I watched the game, I continued to direct my perspectives through those of the players on the field. As the pitcher stood on the mound, I viewed the field as it must appear from his viewpoint. I felt the touch of the ball in his hand and heard the noises of the crowd as they might sound from where he stood. I tried to imagine the sensation of pitching in the major leagues, what it must mean in terms of personal achievement and self-esteem. I imagined sharing the kinesthetic sensations as he wound up that powerful arm and fired toward the catcher. And I shared his quick flash of victory as a signal from the umpire and a groan of "Ste-e-e-r-i-ike" confirmed that he had hit his mark.

It was at that point that I discovered the inherent contradiction between the selflessness of Extro • Dynamics, which brings people together, and the divisive spirit of competition. I looked up at the batter and, quickly coursing through the simple steps, recognized that the victory that I shared with the pitcher was, simultaneously, a defeat to be shared with the batter. The cycle repeated over and over. Each time a batter got a hit, I shared the disappointment in the pitcher and fielders; every time a ground ball was scooped up by a graceful infielder and fired successfully to first base, I shared the satisfaction of the fielders and the frustration of the batter.

When Extro • Dynamics is implemented in a serious way and applied to competitive interactions, it becomes quickly apparent that the success of one competitor absolutely depends on causing the failure of another. As a spectator, sharing the natural flow of consciousness that can be experienced among human beings, I am torn between the joy that I share with the hitter who has hit a two-run homer for a come-from-behind victory in the bottom of the ninth, and the agony of the now-losing pitcher who served it up.

It soon becomes apparent that Extro • Dynamics, so fundamental to joyful success in personal interactions and as the common solution to so many other problems, is severely compromised by competition — the sole purpose of which is for the recreation and entertainment of its participants and spectators. And while it may seem improbable for a chapter on "Competition" to be included in a section on "Contemporary Issues," like Extro • Dynamics itself, this issue has a domino-like effect on other issues.

By applying Extro • Dynamics to recreational activities, you can quickly experience for yourself the inherent contradiction that competition creates, both as a spectator and as a participant.

As a spectator: just as I did, let your natural flow of consciousness link up with those who are playing, on *both* sides. Let yourself feel the perspectives of each team, and experience the constant simultaneous dissonance of trying to celebrate the victory and suffer the defeat that is represented in each progression of play.

As a participant: try playing baseball (or whatever sport you enjoy) in a normal competitive environment, using the steps. Then play again without keeping score. Without a specific goal to "win," you can truly play with spontaneous enjoyment. You don't have to worry about strict adherence to structure or rules, since the outcome doesn't matter. You can allow four or five strikes to younger children, or eliminate strikeouts altogether. You can still celebrate performing at your best, but the reward now becomes true spontaneous playfulness rather than numbers on a scorecard which, in the long run, are not the highest measure of satisfaction or achievement.

Is our American obsession with competition really necessary? The very question almost seems un-American! Writing this, as I am, in the United States of America in the closing days of the twentieth century, it is appropriate that this discussion should conclude with a topic that is central to the ethical schizophrenia of this country.

On the one hand, as noted earlier, we are taught underlying values of love, compassion, cooperation and brotherhood in all of our social and cultural institutions. Yet cooperation is the very antithesis of competition. Cooperation is the process by which individuals work together for common goals — where the success of one is the success of all, and victories are shared. Cooperation achieves results. It is constructive. It heals and builds.

On the other hand, a good deal of the fabric in our day-to-day social system is built on a foundation of competition. Our judicial institutions rest on an "adversary" legal system, in which opposing sides compete to win or lose before an impartial umpire, rather than in working together to determine what is right or fair or best for all; competition is perceived as the foundation of our "free-market" economy while, in reality, those in power only encourage competition among their adversaries, to weaken them, and seek to limit any real competition against themselves, because they recognize its destructive power. Consumers seek to impose competitive requirements (anti-trust controls) as a limitation on commercial pricing policies. When competition intrudes into personal relationships, as it too often does in "the war between the sexes" or foolish rivalries among friends, intimacy is destroyed and relationships impaired. This does not occur in cooperative interactions based on truly unselfish sharing. Competition is the process in which one person succeeds because another person failed. Competition separates and divides people instead of bringing them together. It is destructive. It fosters pain and isolation.

Even in athletic contests, members of the same team — sharing common objectives — work together in harmony, and call it "teamwork." The destructive power of competition is reserved only for those on the other team, the "enemy." Some experts even express concern that the level of competition in sports stirs up increased levels of violence among its fans. Some point to the rape conviction of boxing great Mike Tyson, or football star O.J. Simpson's history of domestic violence and the allegations that he murdered his estranged wife, Nicole Brown Simpson. Then there is the account of soccer player Andres Escobar, Word Cup player from Colombia, who was murdered after committing an accidental "auto-goal" in which he kicked the ball into his own goal, causing his team to lose a "crucial" game. While few athletes carry their macho competitiveness to such extremes, there is concern about the all-consuming desire to win that is bred in organized, competitive sports.

In the United States, to challenge the sacred cow of competition is to attack apple pie and motherhood. Many of the same objections come up over and over again. For a much more detailed study of the origins, psychology and workings of competition, I highly recommend an excellent book recently brought to my attention, *No Contest: The Case Against Competition,* by Alfie Kohn, but for now we may consider some of the common questions:

Competition is _natural_, it's part of human nature
The only reason competition seems to be so natural is that it is conditioned from such an early age in the American culture. In some cultures, notably certain Native American societies, competition in social interactions is not only completely unheard of, but when foreigners have attempted to introduce the concept, the

people have a very hard time understanding or accepting it. Competition is not natural for humans, it is learned. But, like a drug, once it is acquired it can be a tough habit to kick.

Perhaps it originates from trying to survive in an economic environment in which allocation of value is a function of scarcity, and there is a widespread perception that the accumulation of wealth is predicated on a willingness to compete for it.

In any case, even if competition were "natural," there are many aspects of "nature" such as earthquakes or floods or other "natural" disasters that we try to overcome and from which we seek to protect ourselves. Even if this negative aspect of our being were natural to us, then we should try to rise above the worst aspects of our nature and draw out the better side of our character.

Competition is essential to the economy
The "captains of industry" often give lip service to the value of competition, but if they truly valued competition American auto manufacturers would try to encourage more competition from German or Japanese companies or among each other. Yet the only time they join forces cooperatively, as on the issue of international trade restrictions, for a competitive advantage in trying to defeat their common "enemy," such as foreign companies, labor unions or consumer groups. Otherwise, they don't actually encourage a stronger competitive marketplace. Despite their paeans of praise for competition, they know only too well that they are weakened, not strengthened, by competitors.

This is exactly the reason that anti-trust and anti-monopoly laws have been created — without such protection, commercial industries would reduce competition. And, because they perceive an economy based on scarcity, they would prefer to cooperate with each other to compete against consumers for their "scarce" dollars.

Of course, as noted in Chapter 11, "Economic Prosperity," the real source of long-lasting economic success is for producers and consumers of goods to stop seeing each other as competitors in slicing up the "scarcity" of a limited economic pie, and to work together to make a bigger pie; for workers and employers to stop seeing each other as competitors for the limited income received at their common work place, and to bring in more dollars by working together in a cooperative spirit of "Light Management," for sharing a more productive and enjoyable work environment [Basso 1993 & 1986; Also Basso & Klosek].

Competition brings out the best in its participants

Football coach John McKay, head coach of the USC Trojans college team and Tampa Bay Buccaneers professional team, at the height of his involvement and enthusiasm with the sport, observed in a 1973 *Los Angeles Times* interview: "The pressure on a winner becomes obsessive. The more you win, the more you cannot live with the thought of losing .... [A winner] lives in fear of losing.... A winner loses his good humor. That's what happened to me. I don't smile much any more."

Over the past decade there have been numerous reports of injuries and deaths at soccer matches around the world as overzealous fans respond to a building up of competitive frenzy that is more intense than what they are able to control.

Competition is a fiercely intense emotion, yet not a positive one. It is one that sucks the joy out of activities that were designed to be fun. Competitors play to *win,* not for fun. One time when I was about twenty, my twin brother Dennis and I were at a neighborhood park casually tossing and batting around some baseballs. A team of little leaguers was practicing on the next diamond. Dennis and I paused a moment to watch the joy of children at play. We noticed that one of the players, a hopeful but awkward young kid on second base, was having a pretty hard time. The worse things got on second base, the tougher the coach got and the more frustrated the kid became. The coach was determined to make him learn it *right.* Finally, we overheard the kid mumble to the player next to him at shortstop, "Y'know, this isn't as much fun as I thought it would be." Unfortunately, the coach also heard him. He looked up, right toward second base. "I think I heard someone complaining about *fun.* Baseball's not supposed to be *fun* — it's *hard work!* After you learn to do it *right,* then maybe you can have some fun."

The same thing also occurs in other competitive venues. In competitive gymnastics, figure skating, swimming and diving,

190

judges, coaches, and bureaucrats have taken some of the most free-spirited and playful expressions of physical movement that exist and assigned arbitrary point systems that add structure, pressure and a semblance of objectivity to quantifying the freest expressions of human physical art. In beauty contests, competition-obsessed Americans have even found ways to assign point values for such subjective æsthetics as "beauty" or "personality," which can only be evaluated in the individual eye of each beholder, as they entice women to endure month after month of cutthroat pressure through local, state and national competitions to present themselves like slabs of beef to be awarded labels of "prime" or "choice."

Does this mean we should never play ping-pong if someone wants to keep score? I would never recommend a rigid or dogmatic response that causes more friction in real human interactions than what it is intended to prevent. Rules and principles are guidelines, not laws etched in stone. If we are truly in harmony with the spirit of those around us, we can decide when it is best to participate in a friendly, low-key competitive activity and when it is practical to suggest positive, non-competitive alternatives.

We quickly find that alternatives to competitive recreation are readily available. As noted earlier, in many cases we can play the same games as always, modified only slightly to eliminate the element of competition. The level of fun actually increases, because the objective is no longer to *win,* but to *play.* We are more able to celebrate excellence of performance by either team, because a victory by our "opponent" no longer causes us to experience a loss.

In addition to adapting existing favorite sports for enjoyment without competition, there are also alternative games designed specifically for non-competitive play, and there are several excellent publications offering suggestions for innovative, non-competitive sporting and athletic activities. [Orlick 1978; Deacove 1974; Lentz & Cornelius 1950; Harrison 1975]

Achieving victory over the neurotic competitive compulsion of our times is accomplished by incorporating the Extro • Dynamics model as the basis for all our interactions with other people.

Extro • Dynamics enables us to implement practical values of compassion in our personal lives as well as in public policy, while also letting us enjoy all the best that human existence has to offer.

Simplistic? Too good to be true? It works because it addresses root causes, not symptoms. As demonstrated clearly throughout this book, the many seemingly different issues are all inter-connected. While they may appear in very different forms, they all come from the same source.

Whether for our personal success and happiness or the solution of social problems; whether looking at policies to be implemented now or long-range goals for solving our problems by teaching practical lifestyles of compassionate joy to the next generations — the answers lie in learning, teaching and *living by* practical, action-based values of caring and unselfishness.

Chapter 13 Summary

Competitive strategies cause individuals to work *against* each other, while cooperative strategies align common goals and interests for mutual success. Competition puts participants in adversarial roles against each other, contrary to the process of Extro • Dynamics™.

Teaching
Extro • Dynamics

Having learned to feel compassion and, more importantly, to <u>act</u> <u>compassionately</u> in all areas of our lives, we notice our increased cheerfulness and good feelings in all parts of our lives. No matter what others may do to us, we no longer allow them the arrogance of controlling how we choose to feel.

Still, the world would be happier and more harmonious if more people shared the happy feelings of compassionate joy that have brightened our lives. While we don't necessarily need them to reciprocate our compassion, we wish these people whose interests we have come to share and whose feelings we care so very much about could also experience the same compassionate joy.

There are really two aspects to consider in teaching the compassionate joy of Extro • Dynamics: the first is sharing these practical values with adults, who already have lifestyle habits in place that might have to either be modified somewhat or completely overhauled, and the second is in teaching values to children, who are still forming their lifestyle habits and relationship patterns and who can just as easily pick up the habits and feelings of Extro • Dynamics as any other.

Teaching compassion, to children as well as adults, should be the highest priority for any forward-looking civilization.

14

Teaching Children

Real learning, internalized within our personalities to become part of our automatic lifestyle habits, is more than just memorizing facts or ideas. Learning to actually *live by* Extro • Dynamics does not require any of the conceptual ideas from the first three chapters of this book, or a lot of the other explanatory material. It only requires *putting it into <u>action</u> on an ongoing and repetitive basis!* As mentioned earlier, when you look at the lives of people who have developed compassion naturally, they often do not even understand how or why such habits became a part of their personalities. It just happened.

So why did I write all the other stuff? In order for adults to take the active step of overcoming the inertia of their existing lifestyle habits and *do* something different, they usually need a reason. So all the facts, information and reasons are provided to motivate you to get started, and to show you *how,* with practical techniques that fit *your* lifestyle. But even if this approach convinces you, it will not actually benefit you until those ideas and beliefs are translated into ongoing lifestyle habits.

Children respond better to *activities* than explanations. It is not effective to explain the psychology or sociology of happiness. Skip the explanations. Just *do it.* They will quickly develop powers of compassionate joy that will amaze you!

One note: I have often heard the expression, "Children are cruel." Examples abound in which children tease or persecute those who are perceived as being different or who don't fit in smoothly with the dominant social clique.

As the second oldest in a large family, a day-camp counselor for three years while working my way through college, a single parent to my daughter for many years and working occasionally in special projects for underprivileged and abused children in institutional settings, I have been close to many youngsters. And I do *not* agree that "Children are cruel." It is true that, in the absence of positive direction (as distinguished from scolding or nagging), children often tease each other in ways that seem cruel. In most cases this is only because they don't yet understand the cognitive perspective of their "victim," and they are curious about those in whom they perceive differences. Such behavior seems to be associated more closely with the natural flow of consciousness among humans described in Chapter 3, from which the experience of empathy originates, than from intentional cruelty, except in special cases of abuse or emotional trauma where children express deep-seated anger requiring professional attention.

In fact, young children are neither compassionately kind nor maliciously cruel. They are still forming their social attitudes. Some will become mean and violent brutes leading lives neither happy nor joyful; some will become cheerfully compassionate and beloved by all who know them; and most will be somewhere in-between — sometimes compassionate and sometimes not, depending on varying situations, moods and relationships.

Because children begin life as a "blank slate," in terms of their interpersonal values, parents and others who work with children have a tremendous influence over the direction in which their social values will develop. When those who are closely involved with children demonstrate compassionate joy in their own lives, they will find that their young charges easily learn to enjoy the same values. In fact, learning by example is the single most powerful influence in a child's acquisition of the values they actually live by. Children can internalize the steps with greater ease than adults, because they usually have less "old baggage" to unlearn in their simpler lifestyles; they are not distracted by the pressures to earn a living, raise a family and handle the many other responsibilities faced by adults.

In fact, Extro • Dynamics closely parallels the development of human cognition in children. Science writer Morton Hunt details a cognitive model based on the observations of Jean Piaget, in which infants begin life wholly self-absorbed and, with increasing maturity, learn to experience the world around them, incorporate the feelings and perspectives of other people in the surrounding environment (empathy) and to act in accordance with those perspectives [Hunt 1982, pp. 201-206].

Provide a Loving and Nurturing Foundation

While all the steps in the model are important, the first step still comes first. Self-worth and self-confidence are ongoing processes that always operates in the background. If a child grows up without a loving, nurturing and supportive environment, it does not mean he can never achieve happiness. But he will first have to reverse those deficiencies and make up for lost time.

When we express loving, nurturing and supportive affection to our children, we help them build their first step. They learn to feel good about themselves. If we teach them to be aware of their feelings, they learn to celebrate the value of their own consciousness, which is essential to sharing feelings and interactions with others. Children who are nurtured in love learn the skills of love so that, not only do they start out with a solid first step, but they also have the skills of loving that form the basis of the remaining steps.

If we find it hard to express loving, nurturing and supportive affection to our children, we can use our own cheerful lifestyle to overcome feelings of inadequacy, reach out through the perspectives of our little ones, and find the right behavioral response to really show our love. For many who have difficulty with their children, adding this simple model will be enough. For others, professional counseling or participation in support groups may be additional tools of great value. Do whatever it takes. The rewards for both you and your children will be enormous!

Make it Fun! Make it Meaningful!

As described in Chapter 2, "Desires & Values," human consciousness is an active process of mental and emotional energy. It is not static like a physical object at rest. It requires constant interaction with its environment.

The process of learning is one in which the mind reaches for stimulation. The human mind *wants to learn.* It is in a constant search for new information of interest. That is why people who would never watch educational programming on their local PBS station or take a physics class at their nearby community college might still spend long hours reading newspapers, magazines, self-help books, or watching the evening news on television.

Here is something that too many school systems have failed to understand: *children want to learn.* Children at the age of five or six, before they start their formal schooling, are incessantly curious, pestering adults with questions about every imaginable thing. But soon after entering classrooms where they have to sit still for hours at a time, herded into what is essentially a single lesson plan for thirty students that they all have to follow at a uniform pace, they soon decide that their school experience is stale and confining and irrelevant to real life. They not only become bored with school but with anything which resembles their perception of "learning." The insatiable appetite for learning that they were born with gradually fades away until, by the time they become teenagers, their enthusiasm and creativity are often snuffed out entirely by demands for rigidity, conformity and drudgery, and they go through school trying to do the least amount of schoolwork possible while pursuing the social interests which still motivate them.

Of course, there are many exceptions. Some students maintain their fascination for learning throughout their lifetimes and never allow educators to deny them the great pleasure of learning. There are teachers who ignite the spark of fascination in the subjects they teach, and create learning experiences that are not only fun, but which relate in meaningful ways to the students' experiences. Such learning is not only enjoyed, but retained for a lifetime.

Students become frustrated and bored when they have to memorize times tables, yet most young athletes will easily learn to add and subtract to keep scores in their sporting events, and will learn multiplication and division to calculate batting averages and earned-run-averages. Students may have a hard time memorizing letters and phonics, but will happily learn to read if they know they can "have a story any time they want one," or enjoy comic books or sports stories or fantasy adventures (or whatever reflects *their* current interests) while they work their way up to an appreciation of finer literature. High school students who feel that math is irrelevant to real life experiences should be learning how to pay bills, balance checkbooks and figure wages and taxes — not only learning math, but real-life skills they will soon be using every day. Students often become bored memorizing names, dates and places in history and geography, yet they love to watch fictional stories on TV or in movies. If "history" could be presented as true-life stories of adventure and intrigue from the past, and long-past events tied to issues and current news affecting modern life, history and geography would come to life in the same way that, at some point, it did for the teachers who became motivated enough to devote their lives to teaching it.

Educators themselves must learn the simple Extro • Dynamics model, and see the world through the giggly, wiggly eyes of their curious and enthusiastic little ones. They must appeal to the creativity and individuality of their students, to pass along their own fascination for their subjects.

Similarly, in teaching social skills and values, they shouldn't sit kids down and make them learn irrelevant ideas and concepts. They should create innovative projects and activities that touch the individual experience of each child.

Here's an idea that helped me teach compassion to my daughter:

When JoAnn was eight years old, she came home from school one December afternoon, very upset. Some kids had been teasing her because she still believed in Santa Claus. Her Dad had told her there was a Santa Claus, and she knew he would never tell a lie.

"Daddy," she said, "I'm eight years old. I'm old enough to know *The Truth.* Is there really a Santa Claus?" Parents dread this question almost as much as, "Where do babies come from?"

"Okay," I answered. "If you're old enough to know *The Truth* about Santa Claus, then you're old enough to know the truth about the Easter Bunny and the Tooth Fairy as well."

"I want *The Truth.*"

"Well, your Daddy is really the Easter Bunny. And your Daddy is really the tooth fairy. [Pause] Santa Claus is real."

Her eyes grew big and round. "Santa Claus really comes each Christmas Eve and leaves presents?"

I said, "The Easter Bunny and the Tooth Fairy are mythical characters, made-up for holiday fun. Santa Claus is real. He really lived and is based on a real person. But it is often difficult for very small children to understand about the real Santa Claus, so over the years a lot of make-believe and fantasy have been added."

We talked about the historical figure, St. Nicholas, Bishop of Myra, who used to go out on Christmas Eve with gifts for poor children who would otherwise have no Christmas. But like all real human beings, he eventually grew old, and died at the age of 73 on December 6, 343. But after Nicholas, others took up the role. We read together stories from newspapers and magazines of people up to the present day who spread joy by giving Christmas gifts in secret. There are lots of them! Santa Claus is not only real, but alive and doing very well in the modern world.

"If you're old enough to know *The Truth* about Santa Claus," I concluded, "maybe you're old enough to *be* a Santa Claus."

"*Be* a Santa Claus?" she asked, brightening.

It was too close to Christmas to make extensive plans for the current year, but we talked about ideas for the next year.

The following year JoAnn and I contacted the Post Office to receive letters that underprivileged children had sent to Santa Claus. We found that the Post Office believes in Santa Claus, too, and takes its role seriously, and does deliver letters from underprivileged children to real Santa Clauses.

We were able to identify three needy families, and deliver a real Christmas to each one. Instead of random gifts through large organizations for "boy—age 9" or "girl—age 6," we responded to specific requests from individual children. What fun we had shopping, wrapping, and planning a Christmas Eve delivery route — just like any real Santa!

We felt our adventure that first year was successful. All of the children we found were in difficult situations, and it appeared they would have had no Christmas without us. But much of our energy had been spent screening the letters to choose which children were most needy. We also considered that poverty alone is no indicator of whether or not a child will have Christmas. Many families, poor but loving, will make sure their little ones enjoy holiday magic.

The following year JoAnn and I tried a different approach. We located an agency that provides care for children who had been removed from their families on account of child abuse or neglect. A social worker helped us make arrangements to be Santa for six children in a group home who needed a Santa Claus. Over lunch, she told us about each one, and what each child had requested from Santa. Again, we provided the items on their lists, and enjoyed our merriest Christmas ever. We were hooked. We continued this tradition for several years, adapting our routine when my wife Thelma joined our family, and trying different variations such as sponsoring "Santa Claus" for children at Mother Teresa's Missionaries of Charity orphanage in the Philippines.[1]

I appreciate the lessons Santa Claus has taught my daughter, and the values he has shared with her. Our Christmases are celebrations of true joyfulness, and in the truest possible measure of great wealth. I do believe in Santa Claus! I especially appreciate the opportunity Santa Claus gave one father to pass on his values to a young daughter.

Discipline

Compassionate teachers and parents still need to apply thoughtful and positive discipline that responds to the active, energetic nature of consciousness. When inappropriate behavior occurs, it must be stopped. But don't just try to "turn off" the energy. Such efforts would be futile and counterproductive. The energy of con-

---

[1] Mother Teresa is best known for her work in Calcutta, India, but has facilities serving those in need throughout the world, including impoverished areas of the Philippines and other third-world countries.

sciousness never really stops until it dies. Instead, redirect that energy. Say "no" to the wrong behavior, while at the same time providing fun and constructive alternatives you can say "yes" to.

Show Them How — Do It With Them!

Learning is doing. In teaching children the interpersonal skills and values of compassion, it is important to get them into the *action* mode as quickly as possible. Get them started in *doing* the steps, *without explanations or analysis.* And do it with them! Your example is the most powerful teacher, and you will also enhance your own happy lifestyle.

For example, for the first step, let children get in touch with their own experiences. As part of other activities such as driving somewhere, visiting the park, or participating in any recreational situation (but *never* as a separate "learning exercise") ask them about their own feelings. Let them explore and understand their own special and individual value, and their unique perspective of experience. Because the first step of Extro • Dynamics is often an ongoing, background process that does not necessarily require that the remaining steps follow immediately, this exploration and celebration of personal specialness can be shared frequently, as a part of many other activities. In moving on to the second step, moving to a neutral perspective to break free of self-preoccupation and then to the third step of recognizing equal value in others, casually observe another person nearby. It can be anyone — well-known or unknown, or of any age, sex, color or background. In fact, for various practices, it may be of value to involve many different types of people. Wonder aloud about the equal value and specialness of feelings in that other person, and allow a response from the child. After becoming aware of their own special value, children are quick to recognize the same special personal value in others. This leads to a linking up with the perspective of the other person and a merging of personal values. Join your child in visualizing the world from the other person's physical perspective — how objects look to him; how the air feels on his skin; what he hears; what he smells. Imagine with your child what the other person is feeling. What is he thinking? Of course, you don't really know. But you can determine many aspects of mood and sensation, and you can develop an awareness that this person represents a unique experiential perspective which exists in a dimension all its own. You can develop a close bonding with the other person. Your child can develop *and enjoy* a feeling of closeness and compassion for another person. And, of course, you can guide your child to the next step, of taking direct action to contribute something cheerful to the other person — a word, a deed, a gesture of kindness, which follows so naturally from the other steps.

You will find that children are very responsive to this exercise and have little or no resistance to it. It is fun. It is a game. But it allows their interpersonal skills and habits to develop in a direction of compassionate kindness rather than cruelty and teasing. And they will quickly develop an automatic habit of interacting with other people through this pattern of compassionate action, and will initiate behaviors in ways that will surprise you. I have seen it in the raising of my daughter and in working with other children.

Teach children to enjoy kindness by enjoying it yourself while you are with them. Conari Press, publisher of several books and materials on "Random Acts of Kindness" for adults also offers a volume called *Kids' Random Acts of Kindness,* filled with ideas and suggestions of ways children can learn the joy of kindness through *action.* Share it with them!

Children who develop this natural interaction based on a compassionate awareness of others are the ones who learn to reach out to other children who may be a little different and draw them into the social circle. They grow up to be adults whose lives are filled with compassionate and cheerful kindness, beloved by others.

While not wishing to be a boastful parent, the child to whom I have been closest is naturally the daughter I raised as a single parent from her infancy until I remarried when she was thirteen.

At the age of two, JoAnn began attending pre-school. When she was three, her teacher called me aside one day to describe how a childish disagreement between two of the other children had escalated until the entire class was polarized in support of one student or the other. When they asked JoAnn whose side she was on, she answered, "The whole thing is silly. I like everybody." The teacher said JoAnn was able to diffuse the whole problem from the "inside," in a way that an authority figure never could.

At the age of four, another teacher told me how a new child, shy and withdrawn, had enrolled in the school and, having a hard time getting accepted, was teased and ridiculed by others. The teacher seemed powerless to reverse peer pressures until JoAnn, a long-time member of the inner circle, drew the child under her wing and brought her protectively into the social group. At the other child's birthday party some months later, the mother marveled at how much her shy, timid child had opened up and increased her self-confidence in the nursery school.

Throughout her childhood, JoAnn participated with me in social projects and activities. As a teenager, with the usual need for independence, she began to develop her own involvement in homeless and environmental issues apart from me. At fifteen she became a vegetarian out of compassion for animals and to help the environment, leading the way as the rest of the family followed her in giving up meat, poultry and fish. Does this mean she is an idealistic nerd, consumed by "far out" causes at the expense of a fun-filled teen life? On the contrary, she has always remained socially popular, active in gymnastics and other sports, and on the high school "drill team" in her sophomore and junior years.

Going into her senior year, after living in the same house for eleven years and growing up with close friendships, she was stunned to learn that we would be accepting an opportunity to buy a beautiful home in a new community 110 miles away. While disappointed, she demonstrated the depth of her versatility and inter-personal relations skills. She worked hard to keep old friendships intact by writing letters, inviting her old friends over, and going to visit them, while at the same time aggressively seeking activities in which to meet new friends in the new area.

I was surprised by her announcement that, as an incoming senior new to the school, she would try out for varsity cheerleader, competing with local girls who had "paid their dues" on freshman and junior varsity squads. She made it — a tribute not only to her own determination and strength — but also to the fairness and good will of the new school. After daily workouts with the team all summer, by the time school started she had plenty of friends and the change seemed somewhat less horrible. Children who learn to live by practical values of compassion will achieve greater success in all areas of their lives.

Of course my daughter and I occasionally had our disagreements about homework, washing dishes or playing the stereo too loud. But she learned self-confidence, interpersonal skills and an achievement ethic. Upon graduation from high school she found a job, moved into her own place, and became self-sufficient while working and going to school, while keeping in close contact through phone calls, letters and visits. She also made mistakes and had to learn to overcome roadblocks of her own making or just the curves that life put in her way — but she makes the effort to do so. She must have learned something about getting ahead by making a contribution to others: after she had been on her job only six months, she got an offer from another company and her existing employer gave her an annualized increase of 42% to keep her! She also enjoyed similar successes in subsequent jobs. For an 18-year old kid! Am I a proud Papa? You bet! *And I do believe it is possible to really instill in children practical values for a life of success through compassionate joy! [Parent's note to JoAnn: isn't it just totally embarrassing when your Dad writes a book and talks about you in it?]*

[This is not to say that children who learn compassionate social habits will never have any problems. They will. Life is not an "all or nothing" proposition. No human being achieves perfection. Good people sometimes lapse into not-so-good behavior, or fall short, making mistakes or errors of judgment not related to compassion. It will be necessary to guide other areas of behavior, using consistent teaching principles, with appropriate, positive methods of discipline when necessary to address inappropriate behavior.]

Action, Not Just Words

Teaching is more than just *telling*. We only learn from the words we hear or read words when they motivate us to actually *do* something. If I teach a class or a workshop, it is not enough just to talk about ideas. I need to see that students can not only articulate and reformulate what I have taught in their own words and concepts, but that somewhere in that process the ideas that go into their brains are re-directed down through the body and come flowing out of the arms and hands and legs in the form of *action*. When you hear or read something you might retain the memory of it until the next test. But there is something about putting your hands on the physical world and doing something tangible that transforms the knowledge into permanent experience.

Lawyers study the law in law school, but they learn how to become real attorneys after they are hired into a firm and file cases and sit in real courtrooms. Auto mechanics, plumbers and technicians — who are judged by results rather than how many diplomas they have — learn their trades in a shop, not a classroom. Doctors and CPA's can't even be licensed to practice until they have gained hands-on, supervised professional experience.

As noted earlier, explaining the reasons behind Extro • Dynamics should be reserved for later studies in psychology or philosophy. Just do it, don't explain it. Children aren't ready yet to understand how and why it works. You may not understand how or why your car or your television set works when you turn it on, you just need enough knowledge to make it work. It's the same with kids. Just show them what to do and let them have opportunities to enjoy this natural process that leads to real happiness. You will be surprised how fast and how deep their cheerful experience of compassion will develop.

The teaching of compassion-building skills and activities, beginning with self-esteem and moving on to interaction with and compassion for others, should be a part of every children's program. Whether in schools, churches, civic organizations or any other institutional framework, the development of a "kinder, gentler" society in which people contribute to each other instead of cheat and hurt each other depends on teaching children genuine and spontaneous feelings of kindness and goodwill.

Even in the public schools, which must rightfully remain neutral in matters of personal beliefs and values, general values of good citizenship, respect for others and good social skills can be taught. The important thing is to recognize the difference between values that are entirely personal (beliefs, preferences and habits) and general community values that influence the ways we may affect others. When such values are based on scientific, neutral observations from psychology, sociology and philosophy, and do not represent (or contradict) specific cultural or religious viewpoints, they can unify and bring communities together. This approach to teaching values can instill responsible behavioral values in young people while they are still receptive, and before other habits and values arise in random fashion from a lack of direction.

(Some may ridicule the idea of teaching "self-esteem," seeking to portray it as a simplistic "feel-good" diversion from other subjects. But, properly taught as a part of other academic disciplines, genuine self-esteem is essential for personal development and success in other subject areas. Certainly there are cases in which "self-esteem" has been cultivated with inadequate or ineffective techniques. Developing self-esteem must be rooted in something authentic. It must never be replaced by its frivolous, superficial imitator, flattery, that feel-good diversion whose phoniness is easily recognized and causes others to feel degraded if that is all they are worth. In contrast, sincerely identifying real skills, talents and achievements is like a genuine compliment that calls attention to qualities one legitimately admires in another person, in a way that rings true and reminds the recipient of the qualities that he knows best reflect the better angels of his nature. Flattery cheapens and degrades. Genuine self-esteem, built on real abilities and real achievements, resonates in the soul and forms the foundation on which to expand our best attributes.)

Certainly it is true that instruction about values should first be the responsibility of parents and families and the private organizations they choose for that purpose. But when values influence the behavior that will affect the community as a whole, and parents fail to teach a minimum of interactive values, the community has not only a right but a duty to step in and insist that children be taught general, non-denominational values, to maintain the public order and prevent subsequent behavioral disorders that lead to criminal violence and social upheaval.

When parents fail to care for their children or abuse them or neglect them or otherwise place them in danger to themselves and others, the community must step in — not to usurp the role of the parents, but only as a backup and only to prevent our precious young ones from growing up to hurt themselves and disrupt the order and safety of the community.

As noted in the section about contemporary social issues, the "sad shape of the world" will only improve as humans learn and teach deeply-internalized lifestyles of compassionate joy starting from an early age. Children will learn to interact with others one way or another. We owe it to them and to our communities to make it one that allows them to enjoy the cheerfulness of practical compassion values.

Chapter 14 Summary
Teaching is much more than just telling. Teaching values to children requires that we create a nurturing and loving environment in which they become receptive to our communication, and that we show them how to put practical values into action by the ways in which we do so ourselves. Explaining concepts is not enough. Practical lifestyle values must become an integral part of everyday lifestyle habits.

15

Teaching Adults

As noted earlier, real learning of new lifestyle habits does not come from understanding concepts, but from implementing new habits of interpersonal behavior. It's not what you *know,* nor what you *believe,* but rather what you *do.* Knowledge or belief is only valuable to the extent that it sets in motion processes of change in lifestyle habits.

Am I repeating myself? Perhaps that is because there are many similarities in the way adults and children learn values. As with children, the important thing is to take *action.*

There are also differences. Adults do not live in structured environments created and controlled by authority figures such as parents and teachers. Adults must develop their own motivation to initiate conditions that lead to internalizing new lifestyle feelings and habits. That is why we offer background explanatory information — to provide credibility and offer reasons to make changes.

Learning of values by adults also differs from children in that adults have had more years of life experience in which harmful or counterproductive feelings and habits may have taken deeper root. For children it is usually a matter of writing new information on a clean slate; for adults it is more often a matter of unlearning old habits before they can be replaced by new ones.

In Chapter 5, "Making It Work," we discussed the process of incorporating Extro • Dynamics into our daily behavioral routines. While it is not necessary to repeat that chapter here, much of the same process applies in teaching Extro • Dynamics to others, except that we share the process with them.

In working with adults, it is not possible to teach values by coercion, preaching or lecturing. For those who have a desire to learn Extro • Dynamics, but just don't know how, we can provide the information that enables them to do it. We can be there to do it with them, and follow the model together and be a sounding board for working through resistance or obstacles. But we cannot force them to do it until they are ready. Even if it were possible to compel someone to go through the motions of doing the steps, real learning of values cannot occur unless the spirit and feelings of the learner are receptive to the new behaviors. In order to make truly fundamental changes in personality and temperament, a person must *choose* to do so.

This does not mean that we cannot teach the values of compassionate joy to those who are not yet ready. It just means that we must first take the extra step of leading them to a state of readiness. This must be done by demonstrating the attractive and desirable qualities of a lifestyle based on compassionate joy — drawing them freely and voluntarily to embrace it, not by coercion or nagging.

The 11th tradition in most "twelve step" self-improvement programs encourages spreading the message through "attraction rather than promotion." This can be done in many ways. At just the right moment, when a person is dissatisfied with their counterproductive efforts at achieving self-directed happiness, you can offer a positive and constructive alternative. You can demonstrate the many ways in which they can, paradoxically, attain greater happiness, and even enhance their chances of achieving purely selfish goals such as money, romance, and physical well-being, through a lifestyle of unselfish compassion. Of course, such selfish motivations only serve to set the process in motion. Once it is begun we have to help them lose their purely selfish outlook and become absorbed in the happiness they can share with others.

Whether we find our "student" already eager to learn practical lifestyle habits of compassionate joy or we attract them freely and voluntarily to embrace it, the process then becomes similar to the way in which we teach children: demonstrate the steps in an active process of *doing* them in the course of other activities. Find creative and innovate ways to make cheerful contributions to the experiences you share with others. Make it fun. Don't demand perfection. No one starts out perfectly, yet everyone can benefit the first time they do it. And no one ever achieves such mastery that they are beyond further improvement. We are all constantly seeking new ideas and techniques for enjoying the cheerfulness of compassionate joy and in overcoming resistance to the obstacles. However imperfectly, go through all the steps with your fellow learner as well as you can. Only through repetition will the process become an automatic lifestyle habit.

One final note: The recurring "paradox" of Extro • Dynamics, that the more we lose ourselves in contributing to others the more we truly gain for ourselves, also applies in teaching it to others: When we teach others — an activity of *doing* — we solidify and confirm our own internalization of these lifestyle habits! We learn and feel and internalize far more than what we teach.

Chapter 15 Summary

The key to teaching values to adults is in helping them to find practical ways of making those values a part of real lifestyle habits. Explaining concepts or ideas may be valuable to motivate a person to change personal behavior, or to show *how* to make real behavioral changes. But it is in working together and sharing a process of mutual growth in an active lifestyle of Extro • Dynamics that personal and spiritual growth can occur — leading us and those we love to new levels of achievement in health, wealth, love ... and happiness!

Bibliography

Alcoholics Anonymous, (New York: Alcoholics Anonymous World Services, Inc.) 3rd Edition, 1976.

Agatston, Arthur, M.D. *The South Beach Diet.* (New York: Random House, 2003).

Allen, Robert G. *Creating Wealth.* (New York: Simon & Schuster, 1983).

Atkins, Robert C., M.D. *Dr. Atkins Diet Revolution.* (New York: Bantam Publishers, 1972).

Basso, Bob, Ph.D. and Klosek, Judi, J.D. *This Job Should Be Fun,* (Holbrook, Mass: Bob Adams, Inc., 1991).

Basso, Bob., Ph.D. *555 Ways to Have Fun,* (Old Saybrook, Connecticut: Globe Pequot Press, 1993).

— — *Lighten Up, Corporate America!* (Los Angeles: New Breed Press, 1986).

Begley, Sharon. "Three Is Not Enough: Surprising new lessons from the controversial science of race," *Newsweek* (2-13-95), pp. 67-69.

Boley, Jeri. "Tale of Two Sons," *Guideposts* (February 1995) pp. 2-5.

Bukkyo Dendo Kyokai (Buddhist Promotional Foundation), *The Teaching of Buddha,* (Tokyo, Japan: Kosaido Printing Co., 1966, Rev. 1988).

Burtt, E. A. *Teachings of the Compassionate Buddha* (New York: Mentor Books, 1955).

Buscaglia, Leo F., Ph.D., *Bus 9 to Paradise,* (Thorofare, N.J.: SLACK, Inc., 1986).

— — *Living, Loving, Learning,* (New York: Holt, Rinehart & Winston, 1982).

— — *Personhood*, (New York: Ballantine, 1978).

— — *Love,* (New York: Ballantine, 1972).

Carnegie, Dale, *How To Win Friends and Influence People,* (New York: Simon & Schuster, 1936).

Cobb, Florence. "Healing the Hurts," *Guideposts* (July 1985) pp. 1-6.

Conari Press (Editors). *Random Acts of Kindness,* (Berkeley, California: Conari Press, 1993).

— — *Kids' Random Acts of Kindness,* (Berkeley, California: Conari Press, 1993).

— — *More Random Actos of Kindness,* (Berkeley, California: Conari Press, 1994).

Considine, Bob. "Could You Have Loved This Much," *Guideposts* (March 1959) pp. 1-4.

Cooper, M.D., Kenneth H. *Controlling Cholesterol,* (New York: Bantam Books, 1988).

— — Aerobics Program for Total Well-Being, (New York: Bantam Books, 1982).

— — *Aerobics,* (New York: Bantam Books, 1968).

Counts, Alex. *Give Us Credit,* (New York: Times Books, 1996).

Dalai Lama XIV Bstan'dzin-rgya-mtsho, *Freedom in Exile, the Autobiography of the Dalai Lama,* (New York: HarperCollins, 1990).

Dansinger, M.S., Gleason, J.A., Griffith, J.L., Selker, H.P., Schaefer, E.J. "Comparison of the Atkins, Ornish, Weight Watchers, and Zone diets for weight loss and heart disease risk reduction: a randomized trial" *Journal of the American Medical Association.* 2005: Vol 293, pages 43-53.

Deacove, Jim. *Cooperative Games: For Indoors and Out,* (Perth, Ontario, Canada: Family Pastimes, 1974).

Dennett, Daniel C. *Consciousness Explained,* (Boston: Little, Brown and Company, 1991).

Desmond, Edward. "A Pencil in the Hand of God," [Interview with Mother Teresa] *Time Magazine,* December 4, 1989, pp. 11-14.

Diamond, Harvey and Marilyn. *Fit for Life,* (New York: Warner Communications, 1985).

Dunn, Douglas. *Dazhan,* (Oceanside, California: Word Wizards, 1988).

Ellerbusch, Max. "In One Blinding Moment," *Guideposts* (September 1976) pp. 27-30.

Frankl, Dr. Viktor. *Man's Search for Meaning...* (New York: Simon & Schuster, 1984).

Friedman, M.D., Meyer and Rosenman, M.D., Ray H. *Type A Behavior and Your Heart,* (New York: Alfred A. Knopf, 1974).

Gaines, Evelyn. "The Innocent Intruder," *Guideposts* (April 1987) pp. 10-13.

Gore, Al. *Creating a Government That Works Better and Costs Less,* (New York: Penguin Books, 1993).

Grade, Sir Lew. *Man Friday,* starring Peter O'Toole and Richard Roundtree (1975 ITC/Keep Films Ltd., 1975).

Greene, John. "A Most Unusual Request," *Guideposts* (November 1993) pp. 10-12.

Gross, Martin L. *The Government Racket: Washington Waste from A to Z,* (New York: Bantam, 1992).

Harris, Sydney J. *The Best of Sydney J. Harris* (Boston: Houghton Mifflin, 1975).

Harrison, Marta. *For the Fun of It: Selected Cooperative Games for Children and Adults,* (Philadelphia: Non Violence and Children Program, 1975).

Hill, Napoleon. *Think and Grow Rich,* (New York: Fawcett Crest, 1960).

Holbrook, Clyda. "Victim," *Guideposts* (March 1988) pp. 1-7.

Hotz, Robert Lee. "Scientists Say Race Has No Biological Basis," *The Los Angeles Times,* (2-20-95) page A1.

Hunt, Morton. *The Compassionate Beast,* (New York: William Morrow and Company, Inc.) 1990.

— — *The Universe Within,* (New York: Simon and Schuster) 1982.

Kohn, Alfie. *No Contest: The Case Against Competition,* (Boston: Houghton Mifflin, 1986).

Koran: Sûrah II:263; III:134; IV:36, 114; and XVI:90 and many others.

Lao Tse, *Tao Teh Ching,* #XXII, Translation and additional commentary by Archie J. Bahm. (New York: Frederick Ungar Publishing Co., 1958). p. 27. Additional translations also consulted.

Lentz, Theo F. and Cornelius, Ruth. *All Together: A Manual of Cooperative Games,* (St. Louis: Peace Research Laboratory, 1950).

Lilly, Julie and Montero, Tracy *Any Which Way But Meat,* (Sherman Oaks, California: Lilly & Belote, 1989).

Maltz, M.D., F.I.C.S., Maxwell. *Psycho-Cybernetics.* (Los Angeles: Wilshire Book Co., 1960).

Manchester, William. *A World Lit Only by Fire.* (Boston: Little, Brown & Company). 1992.

Maslow, A.H. *Motivation and Personality* (New York: Harper & Row, 1954).

— — *Toward a Psychology of Being.* (New York: Van Nostrand Reinhold, 2nd Edition 1968).

McKay, John. "Home Q & A," Interview by Marshall Berges in the Home Magazine section of *The Los Angeles Times,* 10-21-73, p. 40.

Morgan, Elaine. *The Scars of Evolution.* (Oxford: Oxford University Press, 1990).

— — *The Descent of Woman.* (New York: Holt, Stein and Day, 1972).

Morris, Elizabeth. "Seventy Times Seven," *Guideposts* (Jan. 1986) pp. 1-6.

Muir, John (edited by Edwin Way Teale). The Wilderness World of John Muir, (Boston: Mariner Books, 2001). Editor's introduction, page xvi.

Nelson, Mariah Burton. *The Stronger Women Get, The More Men Love Football.* (Orlando, Florida: Harcourt Brace Company, 1994).

Olson, Bruce with Susan DeVore Williams, "Hostage," *Reader's Digest* (February 1990) pp. 39-48.

Orlick, Terry. *The Cooperative Sports & Games Book,* (New York: Pantheon Books, 1978).

Ornish, M.D., Dean. *Love & Survival,* (New York: HarperCollins, 1998).

— — *Dr. Dean Ornish's Program for Reversing Heart Disease,* (New York: Random House, 1990).

— — *Stress, Diet and Your Heart,* (New York: Henry Holt & Co., 1982)

Ornstein, Ph.D., Robert and Sobel, M.D., David. *Healthy Pleasures,* (Reading, Mass: Addison-Wesley Publishing Co., 1989).

Peale, Dr. Norman Vincent. *The Power of Positive Thinking,* (New York: Prentice-Hall, 1952).

Peck, M. Scott, M.D. *The Road Less Traveled,* (New York: Simon & Schuster, 1978).

Peters, Thomas J. and Waterman, Jr., Robert H. *In Search of Excellence,* (New York: Warner Book, 1982).

Phillips, Kevin. *The Politics of Rich and Poor,* (New York: Random House, 1990).

Podell, Ronald, M.D. *Contagious Emotions,* (New York: Pocket Books) 1992.

Reed, Richard and Janet. *How To Create Love in Your Life,* (Encino, California: Prasad Press, 1988).

— — *52 Unique & Exciting Ways To Meet Your Lover,* (Encino, California: Prasad Press, 1988).

Restak, M.D., Richard. *The Brain,* (New York: Bantam Books, 1984).

Ringer, Robert J. *Million Dollar Habits,* (New York: Fawcett, 1990).

— — *Looking out for #1,* (Beverly Hills: Los Angeles Book Publishers, 1977).

— — *Winning Through Intimidation,* (Beverly Hills: Los Angeles Book Publishers, 1973).

Rivenburg, Roy. "A Cool Crusader," *The Los Angeles Times,* (7-10-94, p. E2, interview with Greg Laurie of Harvest Christian Fellowship.

Roan, Shari. "Abused Women May Be 'Hostages,' " *The Los Angeles Times,* (8-20-91), p. E5, reporting on presentation by Edna Rawlings to the 1991 annual meeting of American Psychological Assn., San Francisco, California.

Robbins, John. *Diet for a New America,* (Walpole, New Hampshire: Stillpoint Publishing, 1987).

Russell, Bertrand. *The Conquest of Happiness* (New York: Bantam Books edition., 1968) Permission of Liveright Publishers, New York. Copyright © 1958 by Bertrand Russell.

Sinetar, Marsha. *Do What You Love, The Money Will Follow,* (New York: Dell, 1987).

Smith, Adam. *An Inquiry into the Nature and Causes of the **Wealth of Nations**.* (London, 1776).

Spielberg, Steven. *Hook,* starring Robin Williams, Dustin Hoffman and Julia Roberts. (Amblin Entertainment/Columbia TriStar, 1992).

Teresa, Mother. *My Life for the Poor,* (San Francisco: Harper & Row, 1985) p. 95.

Upp, James R., Jr. "Getting On With Life," *Guideposts* (March 1992) pp. 30-33.

Van Buren, Abigail. "Dear Abby" column 2-21-89. Universal Press Syndicate. Reprinted with permission. All rights reserved.

Walborn, Richard E. "The Unexpected Bond," *Guideposts* (February 1985) pp. 16-19.

Walford, M.D., Roy L. *Maximum Life Span,* (New York: W.W. Norton Co., 1983).

— — *The 120-Year Diet,* (New York: Simon & Schuster, 1986).

Welch, Pat. "A Common Bond," *Guideposts* (July 1987), pp. 6-9.

Williams, Redford and Williams, Virginia. *Anger Kills,* (Times Books, 1996).

Ziglar, Zig *See You at the Top,* (Gretna, Louisiana: Pelican Publishing Co., 1991).

— — "How To Be A Winner," (Nightengale-Conant Audio, 1990).

Bibliography

Index

ABOUT THE AUTHOR

Douglas Dunn says his greatest achievement was raising his daughter JoAnn (now all grown up and a mother herself!) alone, as a single parent, from infancy until remarrying during her teenage years. He married the former Thelma Mantos in 1987, and through her had the opportunity of becoming Dad to Tracy and Darby in the Philippines. Granddaughters Carina and Ella are Grandpa's special buddies who share many activities with him.

In the spirit of Extro • Dynamics, which emphasizes *action,* Doug has been involved in leadership roles in various civic, community and charitable organizations, as well as special projects benefiting Deaf people and Spanish-speaking immigrants (Doug is fluent in both American Sign Language and Spanish), civil rights, women's rights, homelessness, education and domestic abuse. He also pursues a vigorous regimen of physical fitness through non-competitive recreational and fitness activities.

Doug currently lives in a solar powered home in San Diego County, California, and drives a 100% electric car. He enjoys positive interactions with humans, animals and nature.

Doug has presented lectures and workshops to college classrooms and community groups, in the United States and overseas (primarily in the Philippines through the efforts of sister-in-law Marilyn and others in his Filipino family), teaching others how to implement habits of success and happiness based on the simple four-step model presented in this book.